MASTER CHORUS BOOK

250 Contemporary, Traditional, and New Choruses

COMPILED BY KEN BIBLE

Contents

Lillenas Publishing Co.

KANSAS CITY, MO. 64141

Worship and Praise

1 ## Jesus, Name Above All Names

N. H.

NAIDA HEARN

Je - sus,____ name a - bove all names,____ beau - ti - ful Sav - ior,____ glo - ri - ous Lord.____ Em - man - u - el: God_is with us!____ Bless - ed Re - deem - er,____ Liv - ing Word.

His Name Is Life

CARMAN LICCIARDELLO
and WILLIAM J. GAITHER
Arr. by Eugene Thomas

C. L.

His name is Mas-ter, Sav-ior, Li-on of Ju-dah, Bless-ed Prince of__ Peace._____ Shep-herd, For-tress, Rock of Sal-va-tion, Lamb of God is__ He._____ Son of Da-vid, King of the A-ges, E-ter-nal Life,__ ____ Ho-ly Lord of Glo-ry, His name is Life._____

3

I Exalt Thee

P. S., JR.

PETE SANCHEZ, JR.

Holy Spirit, Thou Art Welcome

4

D. R. and D. H.

DOTTIE RAMBO and DAVID HUNTSINGER

Holy Spir - it, Thou art wel - come in this place. Ho - ly Spir - it, Thou art wel - come — in this place. Om - nip - o - tent Fa - ther of mer - cy and grace, Thou art wel - come in — this place. —

Holy Savior

5

M. L.

MOSIE LISTER

Slowly

Ho - ly Sav - ior, Lord, we — a - dore You;

Ho - ly Sav - ior, Je - sus, Son — of God.———

6 Abba Father

STEVE FRY
Arr. by David Allen

S. F.

1. "Ab - ba Fa - ther, Ab - ba Fa - ther," Deep——with -
2. Fa - ther, Fa - ther, Je - ho - vah Sham - mah, You are the

in my soul I cry.
One who's stand - ing near.

Ab - ba Fa - ther,

Ab - ba Fa - ther, I will nev - er cease to love——— You.

Oh, How He Loves You and Me

K. K.

KURT KAISER

1. Oh, how He loves you and me;
2. Je - sus to Cal - v'ry did go,

Oh, how He loves you and me.
His love for sin - ners to show.

He gave His life— what more could He give?
What He did there— brought hope from de - spair.

Oh, how He loves you; Oh, how He loves me;

Oh, how He loves you and me.

His Name Is Wonderful

8

A. M.

AUDREY MIEIR

9

Come Celebrate Jesus

JOHN ROSASCO
Arr. by David Allen

CLAIRE CLONINGER

Come cel-e-brate Je - sus, come cel-e-brate Je - sus;

The bread and the wine, the mo-ment in time. ___ Come cel-e-brate

Je - sus, the Spir-it that frees ___ us; His ta-ble

has been laid, come now and cel - e - brate ___ Him. ___

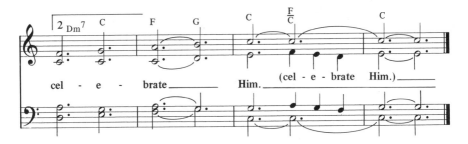

cel - e - brate_____ Him._____ (cel - e - brate Him.)_____

10   **Because of Who You Are**

B. F.

BOB FARRELL and BILLY SMILEY

Lord, I praise You be - cause of who You are, Not be -
cause of all___ the might-y___ things You've done.___ Lord, I
wor - ship You be - cause of who You are; You're all the
rea - son that I need to voice my praise, Be - cause of who You are.

11　　　　　　　　I Live!

R. C.　　　　　　　　　　　　　　　　　　　　　　　RICH COOK

I live, I live be-cause He is ris-en; I live, I live with
I live, I live be-cause He is ris-en; I live, I live to

pow'r o-ver sin.　Thank You, Je - sus! Thank You, Je - sus! Be-
wor - ship Him.

cause You're a-live, be-cause You're a-live, Be-cause You're a-live,_ I live!__

12　　　　　　　Jesus, Lord to Me

G. McS. and G. N.　　　　　　　　GARY McSPADDEN and GREG NELSON

Je - sus, Je - sus, Lord to_ me; Mas - ter,

Sav - ior, Prince of Peace! Ru - ler of my

heart to - day, Je - sus, Lord to me.

13   Fill My Cup, Lord

R. B.

RICHARD BLANCHARD

Fill my cup, Lord— I lift it up, Lord! Come and

quench this thirst - ing of my soul. Bread of heav - en, feed me till I

want no more; Fill my cup, fill it up and make me whole!

14   Let There Be Praise

M. T. and D. T.

MELODIE and DICK TUNNEY

15   There Is a Redeemer

M. G.

MELODY GREEN

1. There is a Re - deem - er, Je - sus, God's own Son;___
2. Je - sus, my Re - deem - er, name a - bove all names;___
3. When I stand in Glo - ry, I will see His face;___

Pre - cious Lamb of God, Mes - si - ah, Ho - ly One.
Pre - cious Lamb of God, Mes - si - ah, O___ for sin - ners slain.
There I'll serve my King for - ev - er In___ that ho - ly place.

Refrain

Thank You, oh, my Fa - ther, for giv - ing us Your Son,___ And

leav - ing Your Spir - it 'til the work on earth is done.

16 Holy Ground

G. D.

GERON DAVIS

We are stand-ing ___ on ho-ly ground, ___

And I know that there are an-gels all a-round. ___

Let ___ us ___ praise ___ Je-sus now. ___ We are

stand-ing in His pres-ence on ho-ly ground.
ho-ly ground.

17　We Are So Blessed

W. J. G. and GLORIA GAITHER　　　　WILLIAM J. GAITHER and GREG NELSON

We are so blessed by the gifts from Your hand, I just
We are so blessed we just can't find a way, Or the

can't un-der-stand___ why You've loved us so much.
words that can say___ thank You,　　　Lord, for Your

touch. When we're emp-ty___ You fill us___ till we o-ver-

flow. When we're hun-gry___ You feed us___ and cause us to

know _____ we are so blessed; take what we have to

bring, Take it all, ev-'ry-thing, _____ for we love You so much. _____

18 O Come, Let Us Adore Him

Traditional

Wade's *Cantus Diversi*

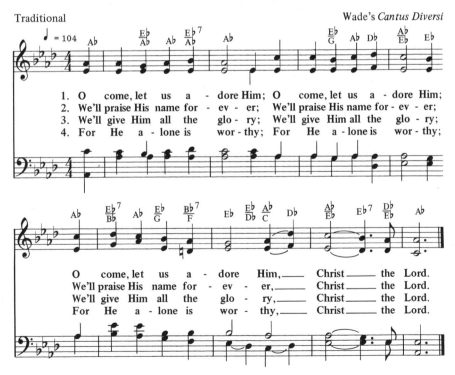

♩ = 104

1. O come, let us a - dore Him; O come, let us a - dore Him;
2. We'll praise His name for - ev - er; We'll praise His name for - ev - er;
3. We'll give Him all the glo - ry; We'll give Him all the glo - ry;
4. For He a - lone is wor - thy; For He a - lone is wor - thy;

O come, let us a - dore Him, _____ Christ _____ the Lord.
We'll praise His name for - ev - er, _____ Christ _____ the Lord.
We'll give Him all the glo - ry, _____ Christ _____ the Lord.
For He a - lone is wor - thy, _____ Christ _____ the Lord.

19

The Lord Is Lifted Up

K. W. and B. C.

KENNY WOODS and BILLY CROCKETT

The Lord is lift-ed____ up in maj-es-ty and__ praise.
Lord is lift-ed____ up, a-bove cre-a-tion__ reigns.

The earth be-holds and bows be-fore the won-der of His__
While earth-ly king-doms rise and fall, His ho-li-ness re-

grace._____ The mains;____ God's ho-li-ness____re-mains.

20

Alleluia

J. S.

JERRY SINCLAIR

1. Al-le-lu-ia, Al-le-lu-ia, Al-le-lu-ia, Al-le-lu-ia,
2. He's my Sav-ior, He's my Sav-ior, He's my Sav-ior, He's my Sav-ior,
3. He is wor-thy, He is wor-thy, He is wor-thy, He is wor-thy,
4. I will praise Him, I will praise Him, I will praise Him, I will praise Him,

Al - le - lu - ia, Al - le - lu - ia, Al - le - lu - ia, Al - le - lu - ia!
He's my Sav - ior, He's my Sav - ior, He's my Sav - ior, He's my Sav - ior!
He is wor - thy, He is wor - thy, He is wor - thy, He is wor - thy!
I will praise Him, I will praise Him, I will praise Him, I will praise Him!

21   King of Kings

SOPHIE CONTY and NAOMI BATYA   Ancient Hebrew Folksong

King of Kings and Lord of Lords, glo - ry, hal - le - lu - jah!

Je - sus, Prince of Peace, glo - ry, hal - le - lu - jah!

Je - sus, Prince of Peace, glo - ry, hal - le - lu - jah!

glo - ry, hal - le - lu - jah!

22   O Magnify the Lord

M. T. and D. T.

MELODIE and DICK TUNNEY

1. O mag - ni - fy,— O mag - ni - fy— the Lord— with
(2. O) wor - ship Him,— O wor - ship Christ— the Lord— with

me, And let us ex - alt His name to - geth - er!—
me, And let us ex - alt His name to - geth - er!—

— O mag - ni - fy— the Lord, O mag - ni - fy— the
— O wor - ship Christ— the Lord, O wor - ship Christ the

Lord, And may His name be lift - ed— high for -
Lord, And may His name be lift - ed— high for -

23   O How I Love Jesus

FREDERICK WHITFIELD   Traditional Melody

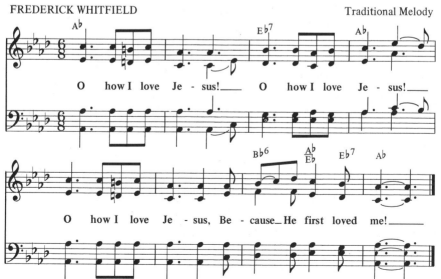

24 We Have Come into His House

B. B.

BRUCE BALLINGER

1. We have come in - to His house and gath-ered in His name to
2. So for - get a - bout your - self and con - cen-trate on Him and
3. Let us lift up ho - ly hands and mag - ni - fy His name and

wor - ship Him._____ We have come in - to His house and
wor - ship Him._____ So for - get a - bout your - self and
wor - ship Him._____ Let us lift up ho - ly hands and

gath - ered in His name to wor - ship Him._____ We have
con - cen - trate on Him and wor - ship Him._____ So for -
mag - ni - fy His name and wor - ship Him._____ Let us

come in - to His house and gath-ered in His name to wor-ship Christ the
get a - bout your-self and con - cen-trate on Him, and wor-ship Christ the
lift up ho - ly hands and mag - ni - fy His name and wor-ship Christ the

Lord. Wor - ship Him, Christ _____ the Lord.
Lord. Wor - ship Him, Christ _____ the Lord.
Lord. Wor - ship Him, Christ _____ the Lord.

25 Worship the King

B. S. and B. G.

BILLY SMILEY and BILL GEORGE

Come, let us wor-ship the King;_____ Je - sus, the Sav-ior, is born._____ For the Lord will reign o - ver all_____ the earth._____ Lord is great and great - ly to be praised_____ through all the earth._____ Let us wor - ship the King._____

26 It's Time to Praise the Lord

B. B. and J. B.

BRUCE and JUDI BORNEMAN

He lives with-in the prais - es____ of His
peo-ple; He loves to hear us call up-on____ His
name._____ So _____ praise the Lord.

27 **Beautiful**

D. C.

DENNIS CLEVELAND

Beau-ti-ful, beau-ti - ful, Je - sus is beau-ti-ful, And Je-sus makes
Care-ful-ly touch-ing me, Caus - ing my eyes to see, ____ Je-sus makes

beau-ti - ful things of my__ life._____ things of my__ life.
beau-ti - ful

28   In This Very Room

R. H. and C. H.

RON HARRIS and CAROL HARRIS

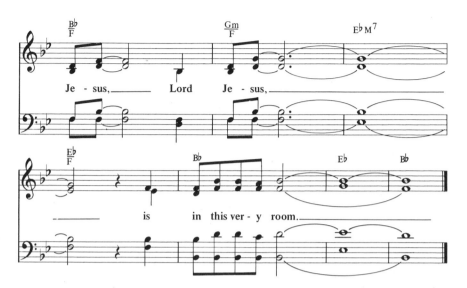

Je - sus,_____ Lord Je - sus,_____

_____ is in this ver - y room._____

29   Honor the Lord

G. D. and G. F.

GREG DAVIS and GREG FISHER

Hon - or the Lord__ with your song of praise, Come be-fore__

_____ Him with sing - ing. Lift up your hands__ and your

voic - es raise; Hon - or the Lord__ with your song of praise.

We Bow Down

T. P.

TWILA PARIS

1. You are___ Lord of cre-a - tion and Lord of my___
(2. You are___) King of cre-a - tion and King of my___

life, Lord of the land___ and the___ sea.
life, King of the land___ and the___ sea.

You were___ Lord of the heav - en be - fore there was___
You were___ King of the heav - en be - fore there was___

time, And Lord of all___ lords You will be!
time, And King of all___ kings You will be!

31 Emmanuel

B. McG.

BOB McGEE

Em - man - u - el, _____ Em - man - u - el, _____

_____ His name is called _____ Em - man - u - el: _____

_____ God with us, _____ re - vealed in us! _____

_____ His name is called _____ Em - man - u - el.

Cornerstone

32

L. P.

I lay in Zi-on___ for a foun-da-tion, a stone. I lay in Zi-on,___ for a foun-da-tion, a___ stone— A tried___ stone, a pre-cious cor-ner-stone, A sure foun-da-tion,___ a sure foun-da-tion, A tried___ stone, a pre-cious cor-ner-stone. He that be-liev-eth shall,___ shall not make haste.

33   Majesty

J. W. H.

JACK W. HAYFORD

Maj - es - ty,_____ wor-ship His maj - es - ty._____ Un-to
Je - sus be all glo - ry, hon-or, and praise._____
Maj - es - ty,_____ king - dom au - thor - i - ty_____
(D.S.) Maj - es - ty,_____ wor - ship His maj - es - ty;_____
_____ flow from His throne un - to His own; His an - them
_____ Je - sus who died, now glo - ri - fied, King of all

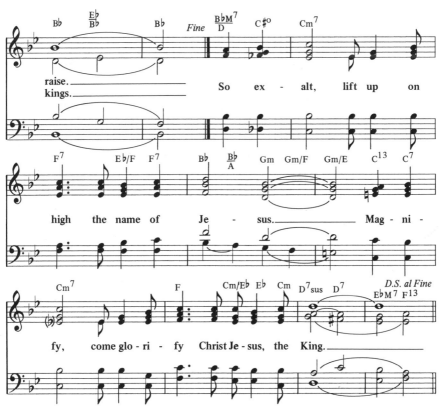

raise._____ So ex - alt, lift up on

kings._____

high the name of Je - sus._____ Mag - ni -

fy, come glo - ri - fy Christ Je - sus, the King._____

34 I Love Him

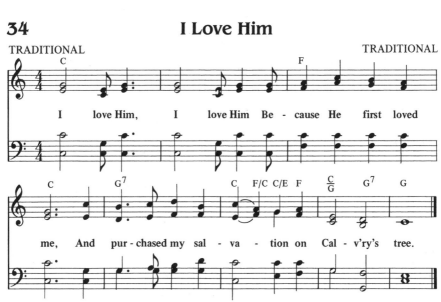

TRADITIONAL   TRADITIONAL

I love Him, I love Him Be - cause He first loved

me, And pur - chased my sal - va - tion on Cal - v'ry's tree.

35 My Tribute

A. C.

ANDRAÉ CROUCH

To God be the glo - ry, To God be the glo - ry,

To God be the glo - ry For the things He has done. __

With His blood He has saved me; With His power He has raised me;

To God be the glo - ry For the things He has done.

Just let me live my life; Let it be pleas-ing, Lord, to Thee.

And if I gain an-y praise, Let it go to Cal va ry. With His

36 ## Let's Talk About Jesus

Traditional

Traditional

Arr. by Lyndell Leatherman

Let's talk a-bout Je sus— the King of Kings is He,

The Lord of Lords su-preme—— through all e - ter - ni - ty;

The great I AM, the Way, the Truth, the Life, the Door—

Let's talk a-bout Je - sus more and more.——

We Will Glorify

T. P.

TWILA PARIS

1. We will glo-ri-fy the King of Kings, We will
ho-vah reigns in maj-es-ty; We will
Lord a-bove the u-ni-verse, He is
lu-jah to the King of Kings, Hal-le-

glo-ri-fy the Lamb, We will glo-ri-fy the
bow be-fore His throne. We will wor-ship Him in
Lord of all who live, He is Lord a-bove the
lu-jah to the Lamb, Hal-le-lu-jah to the

Lord of Lords, Who is the Great I AM. 2. Lord Je-
righ-teous-ness; We will wor-ship Him a-lone. 3. He is
heav'n and earth; All praise to Him we give. 4. Oh, hal-le-
Lord of Lords, Who is the Great I AM.

38

The Love of God

F. M. L.

FREDERICK M. LEHMAN

O love of God, how rich and pure,__How mea-sure-less__ and strong!

It shall for - ev - er - more en - dure___ The saints' and an - gels' song.

39   Let There Be an Anointing

J. H.

JACK HAYFORD

1. Let there be an a - noint-ing of the Spir - it. Let there
2. Let there be a dis - play-ing of Thy glo - ry. Let there
3. Let there be an ex - alt - ing of Christ Je - sus. Let there

be an out-pour-ing of Thy pow'r.___ Let there be an o-ver-flow-ing of the
be a re-veal-ing of Thy grace.___ Let there be an un-der-stand-ing of Thy
be an un-fold-ing of the Word.___ Let the truth bring lib-er - ty of

love of God, That Thy name be mag-ni - fied this hour.
will and way, That Thy king-dom come with-in this place.
life and health, That Thy name be mag-ni - fied as Lord.

40 The Majesty and Glory of Your Name

LINDA LEE JOHNSON
Based on Psalm 8

TOM FETTKE

lu - ia, _____ Al - le - lu - ia, _____ Al - le - lu - ia!

41. Sing Praise to the King

M. L.

MOSIE LISTER

Sing praise _____ to the King of Kings. _____

_____ Sing praise _____ to the King of Kings. _____

_____ Lift _____ high the ho - ly name of Je -

sus; Sing praise, praise to the King of Kings. _____

42 I Will Lift My Heart

D. E. W.

DAVID E. WILLIAMS

1. I will lift my heart in prayer._____ I will lift my heart in prayer._____ To the God who hears His chil-dren pray-ing, I lift_____ my heart._____
2. I will lift my voice in song._____ I will lift my voice in song._____ To the God who fills our lives with mu-sic, I lift_____ my voice._____
3. We will lift our hands in praise._____ We will lift our hands in praise._____ To the God who pur-chased our re-demp-tion, We lift_____ our praise!

43 Thank You, Lord

S. S. and B. S.

SETH and BESSIE SYKES

Thank You, Lord, for sav-ing my soul; Thank You, Lord, for mak-ing me whole;

Thank You, Lord, for giv-ing to me_____ Thy great sal-va-tion so rich and free.

44

I Love You, Lord

L. K.

LAURIE KLEIN

I love You, Lord,_____ and I lift my voice_____

To wor-ship You; O my soul, re - joice!

Take joy, my King,_____ in_____ what You hear;_____

May it be a sweet, sweet_____ sound in_____ Your ear._____

45 Worthy Is the Lamb

Based on Revelation 5:12

DON WYRTZEN

Wor-thy is the Lamb that was slain,_____ Wor-thy is the Lamb that was slain,_____ Wor-thy is the Lamb that was slain_____ to re-ceive:_____

Pow-er and rich-es and wis-dom and strength, Hon-or and glo-ry and bless-ing!_____ Wor-thy is the Lamb, wor-thy is the Lamb, Wor-thy

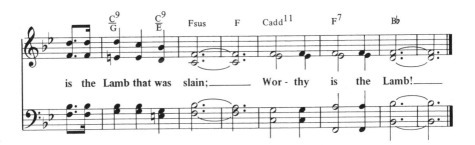

is the Lamb that was slain;_____ Wor - thy is the Lamb!_____

46   We Worship and Adore You

Unknown   Unknown

We wor - ship and a - dore You, Bow - ing down be -

fore You, Songs of prais - es sing - ing, Hal - le - lu - jahs

ring - ing. Hal - le - lu - jah, hal - le -

lu - jah,_____ hal - le - lu - jah, A - men.

Enter His gates with thanksgiving,
And His courts with praise.
Give thanks to Him; bless His name.
For the Lord is good;
His lovingkindness is everlasting,
And His faithfulness to all generations (Psalm 100:4-5).

47   Jesus, We Just Want to Thank You

GLORIA GAITHER and W. J. G.   WILLIAM J. GAITHER

1. Je - sus, we just want to thank You;_____ Je - sus, we just want to thank_____ You; Je - sus, we just want to thank You,_____ Thank You for be - ing so good.
2. Je - sus, we just want to praise You;_____ Je - sus, we just want to praise_____ You; Je - sus, we just want to praise You,_____ Praise You for be - ing so good.
3. Je - sus, we just want to tell You;_____ Je - sus, we just want to tell_____ You; Je - sus, we just want to tell You,_____ We love You for be - ing so good.
4. Sav - ior, we just want to serve You;_____ Sav - ior, we just want to serve_____ You; Sav - ior, we just want to serve You,_____ Serve You for be - ing so good.
5. Je - sus, we know You are com - ing;_____ Je - sus, we know You are com - ing; Je - sus, we know You are com - ing;_____ Take us to live in Your home.

48   His Praise Fills the Temple

J. H.

JACK HAYFORD

Let everything that has breath praise the Lord (Psalm 150:6).

49 Hallelujah!

Unknown

Unknown

Hal-le-lu, hal-le-lu, hal-le-lu, hal-le-lu-jah! Praise ye the Lord! Hal-le-

lu, hal-le-lu, hal-le-lu, hal-le-lu-jah! Praise ye the Lord! Praise ye the Lord, hallelujah!

Praise ye the Lord, hal-le-lu-jah! Praise ye the Lord, hal-le-lu-jah! Praise ye the Lord!

50 A Perfect Heart

D. M. and R. R.

DONY McGUIRE and REBA RAMBO

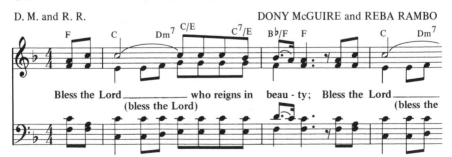

Bless the Lord _____ who reigns in beau-ty; Bless the Lord _____
(bless the Lord)   (bless the

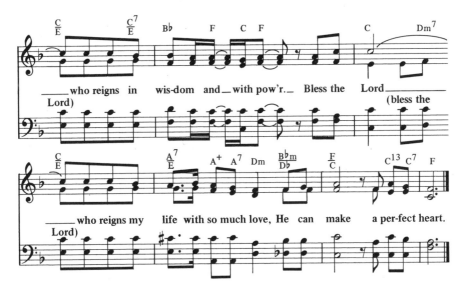

who reigns in wis-dom and with pow'r. Bless the Lord
Lord) (bless the

who reigns my life with so much love, He can make a per-fect heart.
Lord)

51   Bless His Holy Name

A. C.
Based on Psalm 103:1-2

ANDRAÉ CROUCH

Bless the Lord, O my soul, and all that is with - in me, Bless His

ho - ly Name. He has done great things, He has done great

things, He has done great things, Bless His ho - ly Name.

52   # I Will Call Upon the Lord

Adapted by M. O'S.

MICHAEL O'SHIELDS

53 Spirit Song

J. W.

JOHN WIMBER

1. O let the Son of God en-fold you with His Spir-it
   have the things that hold you, and His Spir-it,
2. O come and sing the song with glad-ness as your hearts are
   all your tears and sad-ness; give Him all your

and His love; Let Him fill your heart and sat-is-fy___ your
like a dove, Will de-
filled with joy, Lift your hands in sweet sur-ren-der to___ His
years of pain, And you'll

soul.___ O let Him scend up-on your
name.___ O give Him en-ter in-to

life and make you whole.___
life in Je-sus' name.___ Je-

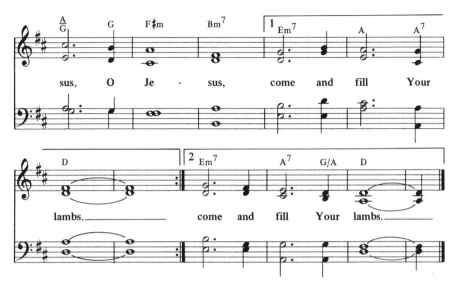

sus, O Je - sus, come and fill Your

lambs. _____ come and fill Your lambs.

54   Jesus Is the Sweetest Name I Know

L. L.

LELA LONG

Je - sus is the sweet-est name I know, And He's

just the same as His love - ly name, And that's the rea - son

why I love Him so. Oh, Je - sus is the sweet-est name I know!

55 Great and Wonderful

S. D.

STUART DAUERMANN

Great and won-der-ful ___ are Thy
D.C. All the na-tions shall ___ come and

won-drous deeds, ___ O Lord God, the Al-
wor-ship Thee, ___ For Thy glo-ry shall

might - y. ___ Just and true ___ are ___
be re - vealed. ___ Hal - le - lu - jah! ___

all Thy ways, O Lord; ___ King of the a - ges art
Hal - le - lu - jah! ___ Hal - le - lu - jah! A -

Thou. ___ Who shall not fear and

glo - ri - fy Thy___ name, O Lord?___

For Thou a - lone art ho - ly, Thou___

D.C. al Coda   CODA

___ a - lone._____ men.___

56   Bless the Lord, O My Soul

Bless the Lord, O my soul; Bless the Lord, O my soul;

And all that is with - in me bless His ho - ly name.

Let's Just Praise the Lord

W. J. G. and G. G.

WILLIAM J. and GLORIA GAITHER

Let's just praise_____ the Lord! Praise_____ the
Lord! Let's just lift our hearts to heav-en and praise the
Lord; lift our hearts to heav-en and praise the Lord!_____

Through Him then let us continually offer up a sacrifice of praise to God, that is, the fruit of lips that give thanks to His name (Hebrews 13:15).

Lord, We Praise You

O. S.

OTIS SKILLINGS

1. Lord, we praise You. Lord, we praise You.
2. Lord, we love You. Lord, we love You.
3. Al - le - lu - ia! Al - le - lu - ia!

Lord, we praise You. We praise You, Lord.
Lord, we love You. We love You, Lord.
Al - le - lu - ia! We give You praise.

O God, Thou art my God; I shall seek Thee earnestly;
My soul thirsts for Thee, my flesh yearns for Thee,
In a dry and weary land where there is no water (Psalm 63:1).

59   I'm Hungry, Lord

Unknown
Arr. by Lyndell Leatherman

Adapted

I'm hun - gry, Lord; I'm hun - gry, Lord; My soul cries

out for ___ Thee. ___ The Liv - ing Bread, the

Wa - ter of Life, The One who quick - ens ___ me. ___

60 This Is My Body

J. H.

JACK HAYFORD

This is My bod-y that is bro-ken for you.
My life for yours,— that your life may be Mine; This

This is the cov-e-nant that Christ now re-news.
bread is My

bod-y;— My blood is this wine. Eat now and drink, Tak-ing

life to your soul; And feast on the prom-ise— let

Je-sus— make you whole. Health for your weak-ness— and for-give-ness— a-

61   **Open Our Eyes**

B. C.

BOB CULL

O - pen our eyes, Lord,———— we want to see
O - pen our ears, Lord,———— and help us to

Je - sus;———————— To reach out and touch
lis - ten.———————— O - pen our eyes,

Him———— and say that we love Him.

Lord,———— we want to see Je - sus.———

62

Behold the Lamb

D. R.

DOTTIE RAMBO

Be - hold the Lamb!___ Be - hold the Lamb!___ Slain from the foun - da - tion of the world. For sin - ners cru - ci - fied,___ Oh, Ho - ly___ Sac - ri - fice!___ Be - hold the Lamb of God! Be - hold the Lamb!___

63 Hallowed Be the Name

L. G.

LILLY GREEN

1. Hal-low-ed be the name (the name) of Je - sus.___
2. Wor - thy is the Lamb, (the Lamb,) Lord Je - sus.___

Ho - ly is the name___ of Je - sus. Oth-er
Righ-teous I can stand___ in Je - sus. We were

king - doms rise and fall,___ but He reign-eth o - ver___ all.___
chained to death, but then___ You raised us up a - gain.___

Hal-low-ed___ be the name (the name) of Je - sus.
Wor - thy___ is the Lamb, (the Lamb,) Lord Je - sus.

I Will Enter His Gates

Leona Von Brethorst

Leona Von Brethorst

I will en-ter His gates with thanks-giv-ing in my heart; I will en-ter His courts with praise. I will say this is the day that the Lord has made; I will re-joice for He has made me glad. He has made me glad, He has made me

glad; I will re-joice for He has made me glad._____

He has made me glad._____

Praise the Lord!
Oh give thanks to the Lord, for He is good;
For His lovingkindness is everlasting (Psalm 106:1).

65   God Is So Good

Unknown   Unknown

1. God is so good, God is so good,
2. He cares for me, He cares for me,
3. I'll do His will, I'll do His will,
4. He is my Lord, He is my Lord,

God is so good, He's so good to me!
He cares for me, He's so good to me!
I'll do His will, He's so good to me!
He is my Lord, He's so good to me!

66

I Will Offer You Praise

G. J.

GARY JOHNSON

I will of - fer You praise___ when the sun meets the dew, And I will
love___

of - fer You praise thanks at the noon's bright-est hue. I will
love

of - fer You praise___ thanks___ when the star - light is due; And if I
love___

wake in the night, Lord, I'll still be prais - ing You.
thank -ing
lov - ing

He Is Life

67

ANON.

LATIN AMERICAN FOLK MELODY

Do not be afraid;
I am the first and the last,
And the living One;
And I was dead,
And behold I AM ALIVE FOREVERMORE,
And I have the keys of death and of Hades (Revelation 1:17b-18).

68 Sing Hallelujah (to the Lord)

L. S.

LINDA STASSEN

Additional verses
2. Jesus is risen from the dead.
3. Christ is the Lord of Heav'n and earth.
4. Praise be to God forevermore
5. Sing hallelujah to the Lord.

lu - jah, Sing hal-le-lu-jah to the Lord.

sing hal-le-lu - jah, Sing hal-le-lu-jah to the Lord.

69 Lift Up Jesus

W. J. and GLORIA GAITHER

WILLIAM J. GAITHER

Oh, lift up Je - sus;____ lift up Je - sus;____ He's the on-ly One can

fill the void in me.____ Just lift up Je - sus,____ lift up Je -

sus;____ He's the on - ly One we real-ly need to see.____

70 Thou Art Worthy

P. M. M.

PAULINE M. MILLS

Thou art wor-thy, Thou art wor-thy, Thou art wor-thy, O Lord,_____ To re-ceive glo-ry, glo-ry and hon-or, glo-ry and hon-or and power._____ For Thou hast cre - a-ted, hast all things cre-a-ted; Thou hast cre - a-ted all things._____ And for Thy pleas-ure

they are cre - a - ted, for Thou art wor - thy, O Lord.

71   Into Thy Presence

Unknown

Arr. by Lyndell Leatherman

Unknown

In - to Thy pres - ence we come, we come;

Not by the works we have done, have done,

But by Thy grace, and Thy grace a - lone,

In - to Thy pres - ence we come, we come. come.

72

Allelu, Allelu

D. W.

DAN WHITTEMORE

Refrain: Al - le - lu,_____ al - le - lu,_____ Song of my
1. Praise Your name,_____ praise Your name;_____ You bore my
2. God of love,_____ God of love,_____ Noth - ing I
3. Prince of Peace,_____ Prince of Peace,_____ All my an -
4. Ho - ly King,_____ ho - ly King,_____ Ex - alt - ed

spir - it in praise_____ to You._____ For all the won-der-ful things_
pen - al - ty and_____ my shame._____ For all the prom-is -es that__
do makes me wor - thy of_____ All that I have in You from_
xi - e - ty now_____ has ceased._____ The bat-tle's o-ver—I've been_
Sav - ior, with joy_____ we sing_____ Glo-ry to God for the hope_

____ You____ do,_____ Al - le - lu,_____ al - le - lu._____
____ I ____ claim,_____ Al - le - lu,_____ al - le - lu._____
____ a - bove._____ God of love,_____ God of love._____
____ re - leased._____ Prince of Peace,_____ Prince of Peace._____
____ You____ bring._____ Ho - ly King,_____ ho - ly King._____

73

He Is Lord

Based on Philippians 2:11

Unknown

He is Lord, He is Lord! He is ris - en from the dead and He is Lord!

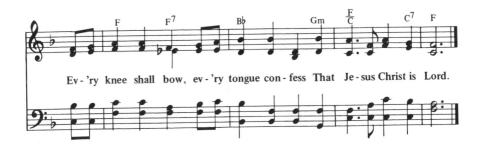

Ev-'ry knee shall bow, ev-'ry tongue con-fess That Je-sus Christ is Lord.

74   Holy, Holy

JIMMY OWENS

J. O.

1. Ho-ly,   ho-ly,   ho-ly,   ho-ly, ___ Ho-ly,   ho-ly, ___
2. Gra-cious   Fa-ther,   Gra-cious   Fa-ther, ___ We're so   blest to be Your
3. Pre-cious   Je-sus,   Pre-cious   Je-sus, ___ We're so   glad that You've re-
4. Ho-ly   Spir-it,   Ho-ly   Spir-it, ___ Come and   fill our hearts a-
5. Hal-le - lu-jah,   Hal-le - lu-jah, ___ Hal-le - lu-   jah, ___

___ Lord God Al - might - y;   And we lift our hearts be-fore You as a
chil-dren, Gra-cious Fa - ther; And we lift our heads be-fore You as a
deemed us, Pre-cious Je - sus;   And we lift our hands be-fore You as a
new, ___   Ho - ly   Spir - it; And we lift our voice be-fore You as a
___   Hal-le - lu - jah;   And we lift our hearts be-fore You as a

tok-en   of   our   love,   Ho-ly,   ho-ly,   ho-ly ho - ly.
tok-en   of   our   love,   Gra-cious   Fa-ther,   Gra-cious Fa - ther.
tok-en   of   our   love,   Pre-cious   Je - sus,   Pre-cious Je - sus.
tok-en   of   our   love,   Ho-ly   Spir-it,   Ho-ly Spir - it.
tok-en   of   our   love,   Hal-le - lu-jah,   Hal-le - lu - jah.

75 Alleluia to the King

M. L.

MOSIE LISTER

O come, let us sing for joy to the Lord;
Let us shout joyfully to the rock of our salvation.
For the Lord is a great God,
And a great King above all gods.

Come, let us worship and bow down;
Let us kneel before the Lord our Maker.
For He is our God,
And we are the people of His pasture, and the sheep of His hand (Psalm 95:1, 3, 6-7).

76

He Is the Way

(He Is the Truth; He Is the Life)

O. S.

OTIS SKILLINGS

1. God sent His Son to be our Sav - ior;_____ God sent His Son_____ to be our Sav - ior;_____ God sent His Son_____ to be our Sav - ior_____ He is the
2. 'Twas Je - sus Christ who came to save the world;_____ 'Twas Je - sus Christ_____ who came to save the world;_____ 'Twas Je - sus Christ_____ who came to save_____ the world._____ He is the
3. He gave His life that we might be set free;_____ He gave His life_____ that we might be set free;_____ He gave His life_____ that we might be_____ set free._____ He is the
4. Rose from the grave that we might live a - gain;_____ Rose from the grave_____ that we might live a - gain;_____ Rose from the_____ that we might live_____ a - gain._____ He is the
5. He lives to - day; I know He al - ways will._____ He lives to - day;_____ I know He al - ways will._____ He lives to - day;_____ I know he al - ways will.

Way; He is the Truth; He is the Life._____
Way; He is the Truth; He is the Life. _____
Way; He is the Truth; He is the Life. _____
Way; He is the Truth; He is the Life._____

_____ He is the Way;   He is the Truth;

He is the Life._____

77   Come into His Presence

Unknown   **(Round)**   Unknown

Come in - to His pres - ence sing - ing   Al - le - lu - ia,
Praise the Lord to - geth - er sing - ing   Wor - thy the Lamb,
                                         Je - sus is Lord,
                                         Glo - ry to God,

al - le - lu - ia,   al - le - lu - ia.
Je - sus is Lord,   Je - sus is Lord.
wor - thy the Lamb,   wor - thy the Lamb.
glo - ry to God,   glo - ry to God.

78 The Lord Is in This Place

M. L.

MOSIE LISTER

Clap Your Hands

79

Adapted from Psalm 47:1 by J. O.

JIMMY OWENS

Clap your hands, all you peo - ple; Shout un - to God with a
voice of tri - umph! Clap your hands, all you peo - ple;
Shout un - to God with a voice of praise! Ho - san - na! Ho -
san - na! Shout un - to God with a voice of tri - umph!
Praise Him! Praise Him! Shout un - to God with a voice of praise!

*May be used as a round.

80   I Saw the Lord

Adapted from Isaiah 6:1, 3

Unknown
Arr. by Tom Fettke

I saw the Lord, I saw the Lord. He was high and lift-ed up and His
train filled the tem-ple; He was high and lift-ed up and His train filled the temple. The
angels cried, "Ho-ly!" The an-gels cried, "Ho-ly!" The angels cried, "Holy is the Lord!"

81   Father, I Adore You

T. C.

*(Round)

TERRYE COELHO

1. Fa - ther,
2. Je - sus, I a - dore You; Lay my life be -
3. Spir - it,

*The accompaniment is optional. When the song is sung as a round, the accompaniment should proba-
bly be omitted.

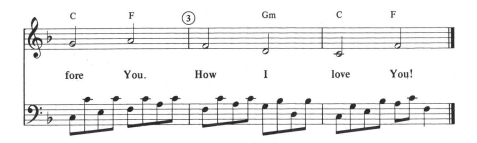

fore You. How I love You!

In this is love, not that we loved God, but that He loved us and sent His Son
to be the propitiation for our sins (1 John 4:10).

82   Father, We Thank You

G. J.

GARY JOHNSON

1. Fa - ther, we thank You; Fa -
2. Je - sus, we thank You; Je -
3. Fa - ther, we love You; Fa -

ther, we thank You for giv - ing to
sus, we thank You for giv - ing to
ther, we love You be - cause You have

us Your Son;____ Fa - ther, we thank You.
us Your Spir - it; Je - sus, we thank You.
first loved us;____ Fa - ther, we love You.

The Lord is my light and my salvation;
Whom shall I fear?
The Lord is the defense of my life;
Whom shall I dread? (Psalm 27:1)

83
S. D.

Behold

STUART DAUERMANN

84   I Will Sing of the Mercies

Adapted from Psalm 89:1

Unknown
Arr. by David Cole

85 Thy Loving Kindness

Adapted

HUGH MITCHELL

1. Thy lov-ing kind-ness is bet-ter than life._____ Thy lov-ing
2. I lift my hands, Lord, un-to__ Thy name._____ I lift my

kind-ness is bet-ter than life. My lips shall praise Thee, thus will I
hands, Lord, un-to__ Thy name. My lips shall praise Thee, thus will I

bless Thee_____ I will lift up my hands un-to Thy Name._____
bless Thee_____ I will lift up my hands un-to Thy Name._____

Because Thy lovingkindness is better than life,
My lips will praise Thee.
So I will bless Thee as long as I live (Psalm 63:3-4).

86 Jesus, I Love You

O. S.

OTIS SKILLINGS

1. Je - sus, I love_____ You, love_____ You, love_____ You.
2. Je - sus, I serve_____ You, serve_____ You, serve_____ You.
3. Je - sus, I praise_____ You, praise_____ You, praise_____ You.

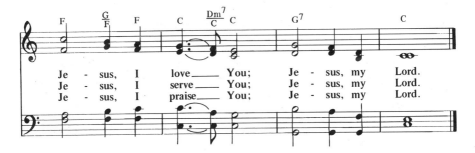

Je - sus, I love___ You; Je - sus, my Lord.
Je - sus, I serve___ You; Je - sus, my Lord.
Je - sus, I praise___ You; Je - sus, my Lord.

Walk in a manner worthy of the calling with which you have been called, with humility and gentleness, with patience, showing forbearance to one another in love, being diligent to preserve the unity of the Spirit in the bond of peace.

There is one body and one Spirit, just as also you were called in one hope of your calling; one Lord, one faith, one baptism, one God and Father of all who is over all and through all and in all (Ephesians 4:1-6).

87 The Bond of Love

OTIS SKILLINGS

O. S.

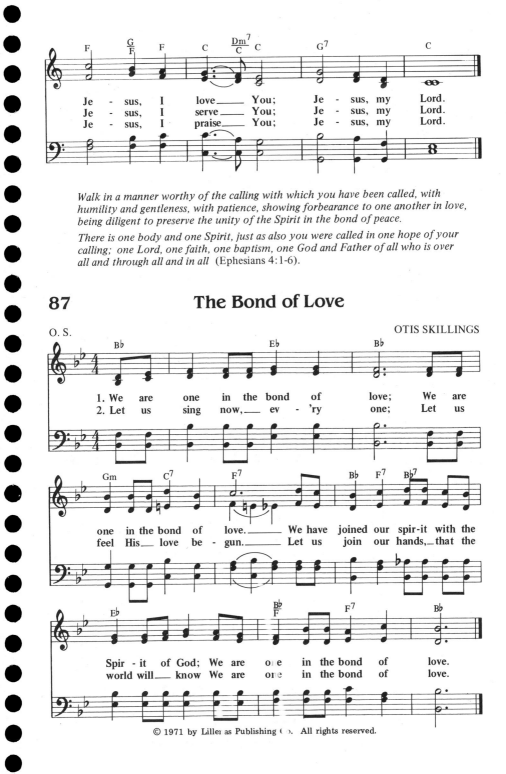

1. We are one in the bond of love; We are one in the bond of love.___ We have joined our spir-it with the Spir - it of God; We are one in the bond of love.

2. Let us sing now,___ ev - 'ry one; Let us feel His___ love be - gun.___ Let us join our hands,___ that the world will___ know We are one in the bond of love.

88 The Heavens Declare

D. L. B.

DAVID L. BURKUM

The heav-ens de-clare___ the glo-ry of God;___ The sky pro-claims the

work of His hands._____ The heav-ens de - clare___ the

glo - ry of God;___ The sky pro-claims the work of His hands.___
1. They
2. Their

speak of the Lord___ day af - ter day,___ Night af - ter night__
voic - es go out___ to all of the earth;___ No lan - guage is known

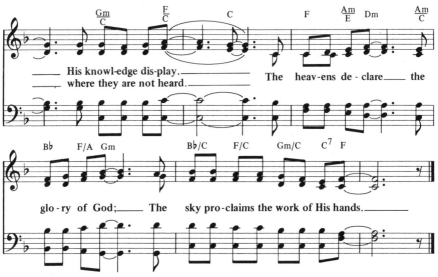

His knowl-edge dis-play.___
where they are not heard.___ The heav-ens de-clare___ the glo-ry of God;___ The sky pro-claims the work of His hands.___

89   Praise Him

Traditional

Arr. by Lyndell Leatherman

Praise___ Him, praise___ Him, ___ Praise Him in the morn - ing, praise Him at the noon - time. Praise___ Him,___ praise___ Him,___ Praise Him when the sun goes down.

Additional verses: 2. Love Him 3. Serve Him 4. Thank Him

90 **We've Come, O Lord**

D. N.

DON NEUFELD

91   Even So, Come

GARY JOHNSON

G. J.

1, 4. E - ven so,   come,_____ Mar - an - a - tha;_____
2. E - ven so,   come,_____ Light   of   men;_____
3. E - ven so,   come, _____ by   Thy   Spir - it:_____

Come,_____ come, Lord   Je - sus._____ The
Come,_____ come, Lord   Je - sus._____ To
Come,_____ come, Lord   Je - sus._____ Up -

Spir - it   and   the   Bride   say,   "Come."_____
those   who   walk   in   dark - ness,   come._____
on   our   sons   and   daugh - ters,   come._____

_____ Come, Lord   Je - sus._____
_____ Come, Lord   Je - sus._____
_____ Come, Lord   Je - sus._____

Rejoicing and Testimony

92

Spring Up, O Well

Unknown
Arr. by Lyndell Leatherman

Adapted

I've got a riv-er of life flow-ing out of me;

Makes the lame to walk and the blind to see, ___

O-pens pris-on doors, sets the cap-tives free.

93 I'm in This Church

J. H.

JOEL HEMPHILL

I'm in this church, this glo-ri-ous church; I did-n't join, oh, I was born; I've had a new birth! Some glo-ri-ous day, gon-na sail a-way; It's by His grace, not by my works I'm in this church!

94 My Sins Are Gone

H. G.

HELEN GRIGGS

Gone, gone, gone, gone! Yes, my sins are gone. Now my soul is free and in my

heart's a song.— Bur-ied in the deep-est sea, Yes, that's good e-nough for me.

I shall live e - ter - nal - ly; Praise God, my sins are gone!

95　Down in My Heart

G. W. C.

GEORGE W. COOKE

1. I have the joy,— joy,— joy,— joy— down in my heart,
2. I have the peace that pass-eth un - der-stand-ing down in my heart,
3. I have the love of Je - sus, love of Je - sus down in my heart,

down in my heart, down in my heart. I have the joy,— joy,—
down in my heart, down in my heart. I have the peace that pass-eth
down in my heart, down in my heart. I have the love of Je - sus,

joy,— joy— down in my heart, down in my heart to stay.
un - der-stand-ing down in my heart, down in my heart to stay.
love of Je - sus down in my heart, down in my heart to stay.

The Happy Side of Life

E. S.

EDDIE SMITH

hap - py side of, I've found the hap - py side of life.

97   Saved to Tell Others

Hollywood Gospel Team

ARTHUR WOOLSEY

We're saved, saved to tell oth - ers of the Man of Gal - i - lee.

Saved, saved to live dai - ly for the Christ of Cal - va - ry.

Saved, saved to in - vite you to His sal - va - tion free.

We're saved, saved, saved by His blood for all e - ter - ni - ty.

98 He Is My Everything

99   His Banner over Me Is Love

Based on Song of Solomon 2:4,
Psalm 40:2, John 15:5
Anonymous

Unknown
Arr. by Lyndell Leatherman

1. I'm feast-ing ___ at His ___ ban-quet-ing ___ ta - ble; His ban-ner o - ver me is love. I'm feast-ing ___ at His ___ ban-quet-ing ___ ta - ble; His ban-ner o - ver me is love. I'm feast-ing ___ at the ___ ban-quet-ing ___ ta - ble; His ban-ner o - ver me is love, His ban - ner o - ver me ___ is love.

2. He placed my ___ feet on the firm ___ foun - da-tion; His ban-ner o - ver me is love. He placed my ___ feet on the firm ___ foun - da-tion; His ban-ner o - ver me is love. He placed my ___ feet on the firm ___ foun - da - tion; His ban-ner o - ver me is love, His ban - ner o - ver me ___ is love.

3. ___ He is the vine and ___ we ___ are the branch-es; His ban-ner o - ver me is love. ___ He is the vine and ___ we ___ are the branch-es; His ban-ner o - ver me is love. ___ He is the vine and ___ we ___ are the branch-es; His ban-ner o - ver me is love, His ban - ner o - ver me ___ is love.

100 I'm So Happy

S. W. G.

STANTON W. GAVITT

I'm so hap-py and here's the rea-son why— Je-sus took my bur-dens all a-way._____ Now I'm sing-ing as the days go by— Je-sus took my bur-dens all a-way. Once my heart was heav-y with a load of sin; Je-sus took the load and gave me peace with-in._____

101 The Longer I Serve Him

W. J. G.

WILLIAM J. GAITHER

The long-er I serve Him, the sweet-er He grows; The more that I

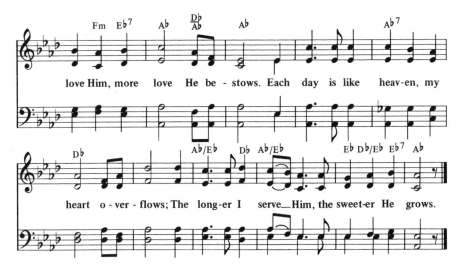

love Him, more love He be-stows. Each day is like heav-en, my

heart o-ver-flows; The long-er I serve—Him, the sweet-er He grows.

102 I'm So Glad

Unknown
Arr. by Mosie Lister

Unknown

1. ___ I'm so glad Je-sus lift-ed me. ___ I'm so glad
2. ___ I was bound, Je-sus set me free. ___ I was bound,
3. I'll tell the world Je-sus lift-ed me. I'll tell the world

Je-sus lift-ed me. ___ I'm so glad_____ Je-sus lift-ed
Je-sus set me free. ___ I was bound,_____ Je-sus set me
Je-sus lift-ed me. I'll tell the world_____ Je-sus lift-ed

me;
free; Sing-ing glo-ry, hal-le-lu-jah, Je-sus lift-ed me!
me;

103   I've Discovered the Way of Gladness

F. W. H.

FLOYD W. HAWKINS

I've dis-cov-ered the way of glad-ness, I've dis-cov-ered the
way of joy, I've dis-cov-ered re-lief from sad-ness:
'Tis a hap-pi-ness with-out al-loy. I've dis-cov-ered the
fount of bless-ing, I've dis-cov-ered the liv-ing Word.___ 'Twas the
great-est of all dis-cov-er-ies When I found Je-sus, my Lord.

104 All Because of Calvary

W. P. L.

WENDELL P. LOVELESS

All my sins are gone,——— All be-cause of Cal - va -
All my sins are gone be-cause of Cal - va -

ry;——— Life is filled with song,——— All be-cause of
ry;——— Life is filled with song be-cause of

Cal - va - ry;——— Christ my Sav - ior lives,———
Cal - va - ry;——— Christ my Sav - ior

Lives from sin to set me free;——— Some day He's com-ing— O
Lives from sin to set me free;———

won-drous bless-ed day! All, yes, all be-cause of Cal - va - ry.———

Go therefore and make disciples of all nations (Matthew 28:19).

105   **Everybody Ought to Know**

Unknown   Unknown

106   **Oh Say, but I'm Glad**

REV. JAMES P. SULLIVAN   MILDRED SULLIVAN LACOUR

107 There's a New Song in My Heart

J. W. P.

JOHN W. PETERSON

There's a new song in my heart since the Sav-ior set me free; There's a
new song in my heart— 'tis a heav'n-ly har-mo-ny! All my
sins are washed a-way in the blood of Cal-va-ry; O what
peace and joy noth-ing can des-troy—There's a new song in my heart.

108 Isn't the Love of Jesus Something Wonderful?

J. W. P.

JOHN W. PETERSON

Is-n't the love of Je-sus some-thing won-der-ful,_____

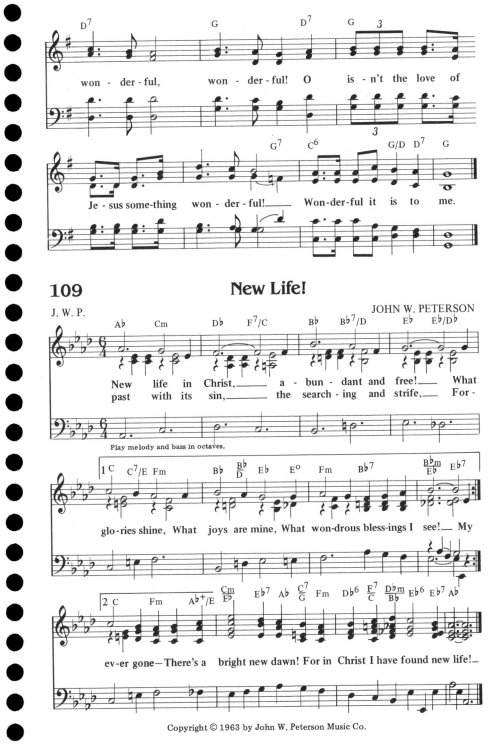

won - der - ful, won - der - ful! O is - n't the love of

Je - sus some-thing won - der - ful!___ Won-der-ful it is to me.

109   New Life!

J. W. P.

JOHN W. PETERSON

New life in Christ,___ a - bun - dant and free!___ What
past with its sin,___ the search - ing and strife,___ For -

Play melody and bass in octaves.

glo-ries shine, What joys are mine, What won-drous bless-ings I see!_ My

ev-er gone—There's a bright new dawn! For in Christ I have found new life!_

110   I'm Gonna Keep on Singing

A. C.

ANDRAE CROUCH

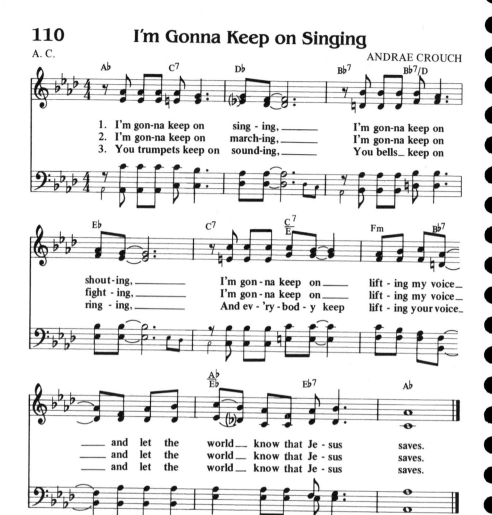

1. I'm gon-na keep on   sing - ing, _____   I'm gon-na keep on
2. I'm gon-na keep on   march-ing, _____   I'm gon-na keep on
3. You trumpets keep on   sound-ing, _____   You bells_ keep on

shout-ing, _____   I'm gon - na keep on ____   lift - ing my voice_
fight - ing, _____   I'm gon - na keep on ____   lift - ing my voice_
ring - ing, _____   And ev - 'ry - bod - y keep   lift - ing your voice_

____ and let the   world_ know that Je - sus   saves.
____ and let the   world_ know that Je - sus   saves.
____ and let the   world_ know that Je - sus   saves.

111   We Have Not Received

Adapted

CHARLES A. TINDLEY
Arr. by Lyndell Leatherman

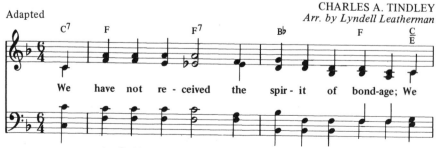

We   have   not   re - ceived   the   spir - it   of   bond-age; We

have not re-ceived the spir-it of fear. But by His Spir-it we

cry, "Ab-ba, Fa-ther." We're joint heirs with Christ and the chil-dren of God.

112   For God So Loved the World

FRANCES TOWNSEND   ALFRED B. SMITH

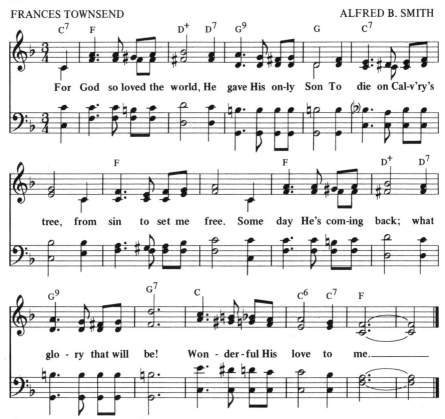

For God so loved the world, He gave His on-ly Son To die on Cal-v'ry's

tree, from sin to set me free. Some day He's com-ing back; what

glo-ry that will be! Won-der-ful His love to me.

This day is holy to our Lord. Do not be grieved,
for the joy of the Lord is your strength (Nehemiah 8:10).

113   The Joy of the Lord

A. G. V.

ALLIENE G. VALE

1. The joy_____ of the Lord_____ is my strength; The joy_____ of the Lord_____ is my strength; The joy_____ of the Lord_____ is my strength; The_____
2. He gives me liv-ing wa-ter and I thirst no more; He gives me liv-ing wa-ter and I thirst no more; He gives me liv-ing wa-ter and I thirst no more; The_____
3. The word of faith is nigh thee, e-ven in thy mouth; The word of faith is nigh thee, e-ven in thy mouth; The word of faith is nigh thee, e-ven in thy mouth; The_____

joy___ of the Lord___ is my strength.___
joy___ of the Lord___ is my strength.___
joy___ of the Lord___ is my strength.___

114   The Family of God

W. J. and GLORIA GAITHER

WILLIAM J. GAITHER

I'm so glad I'm a part of the fam - 'ly of God—

I've been washed in the foun - tain, cleansed by His blood!

Joint heirs with Je - sus as we trav - el this sod; For I'm

part of the fam - 'ly, the fam - 'ly of God.___

115 Behold, What Manner of Love

Adapted by P. V. T.

PAT Van TINE

Be - hold, what man-ner of love the Fa-ther has giv-en un-to us. Be - hold, what man-ner of love the Fa-ther has giv-en un-to us That we should be called the sons of God, That we should be called the sons of God.

116 Happiness

W. J. G.

WILLIAM J. GAITHER

I found hap-pi-ness, I found peace of mind; I found the joy of liv-ing, per-fect love sub-lime; I found real con-tent-ment, hap-py liv-ing in ac-cord; I found hap-pi-ness all the time, won-der-ful peace of mind, when I found the Lord.

117 Soon and Very Soon

A. C.

ANDRAE CROUCH

1. Soon and ver - y soon ___ we are goin' to see the King. ___
2. No more cry - in' there, ___ we are goin' to see the King. ___
3. No more dy - in' there, ___ we are goin' to see the King. ___
4. Soon and ver - y soon ___ we are goin' to see the King. ___

Soon and ver - y soon ___ we are goin' to see the King. ___
No more cry - in' there, ___ we are goin' to see the King. ___
No more dy - in' there, ___ we are goin' to see the King. ___
Soon and ver - y soon ___ we are goin' to see the King. ___

Soon and ver - y soon ___ we are goin' to see the King. ___
No more cry - in' there, ___ we are goin' to see the King. ___ Hal-le-
No more dy - in' there, ___ we are goin' to see the King. ___
Soon and ver - y soon ___ we are goin' to see the King. ___

lu - jah, ___ Hal - le - lu - jah, ___ we're goin' to see the King! ___

Lift up your heads, because your redemption is drawing near (Luke 21:28).

118 Coming Again

M. L.
Based on 1 Thessalonians 4:16-17;
1 John 3:2; Revelation 1:7

MOSIE LISTER

1. Je - sus is com - ing; Je - sus is com - ing;
2. In clouds of glo - ry, Bright clouds of glo - ry,
3. We'll rise to meet Him, Rise up to meet Him;
4. We shall be like Him; We shall be like Him;
5. Oh, hal - le - lu - jah! Oh, hal - le - lu - jah!

Je - sus is com - ing. He's com - ing a - gain.
In clouds of glo - ry He's com - ing a - gain.
We'll rise to meet Him. He's com - ing a - gain.
We shall be like Him. He's com - ing a - gain.
Oh, hal - le - lu - jah! He's com - ing a - gain.

119 Because He Lives

W. J. and GLORIA GAITHER

WILLIAM J. GAITHER

Be-cause He lives___ I can face to - mor-row;___ Be-cause He lives___ all fear is gone;___ Be-cause I know___ He holds the fu - ture,___ And life is worth the liv - ing just be-cause He lives.___

I count all things to be loss in view of the surpassing value of knowing Christ Jesus my Lord (Philippians 3:8).

120 He's All I Need

Traditional

Traditional

1. He's all I need, He's all I need; Je - sus is all I need.___
2. He's real to me, He's real to me; Je - sus is real to me.___

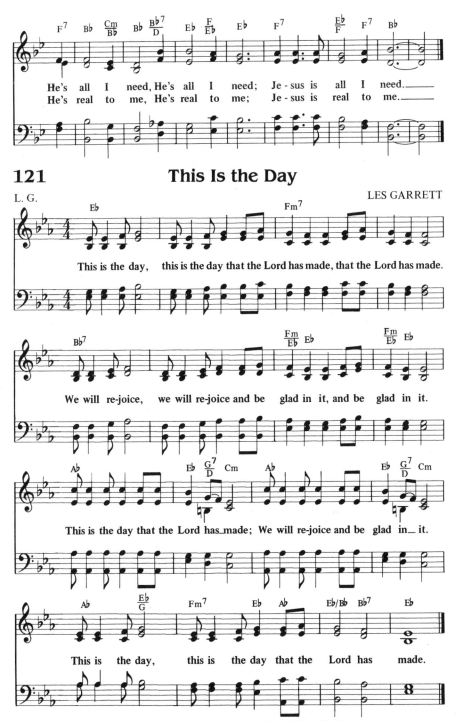

He's all I need, He's all I need; Je-sus is all I need.___
He's real to me, He's real to me; Je-sus is real to me.___

121   This Is the Day

L. G.

LES GARRETT

This is the day,   this is the day that the Lord has made, that the Lord has made.

We will re-joice,   we will re-joice and be   glad in it, and be   glad in it.

This is the day that the Lord has_made; We will re-joice and be   glad in_ it.

This is   the day,   this is   the day that the   Lord has   made.

122   I Am Loved

W. J. and GLORIA GAITHER   WILLIAM J. GAITHER

I am loved, I am loved, I can risk lov-ing you;
loved, I am loved; Won't you please take my hand?

For the One who knows me best loves me most.
We are free to love each

I am
oth-er, we are loved.

123   Isn't He Wonderful

Traditional
Arr. by Lyndell Leatherman

Traditional

Is-n't He won-der-ful, won-der-ful, won-der-ful; Is-n't

Je - sus my Lord won-der - ful! Eyes have seen, ears have heard; 'Tis re-

cord-ed in God's Word. Is - n't Je - sus my Lord won-der - ful!

124   Go, Tell It on the Mountain

Spiritual   Spiritual

Go,   tell it on the moun - tain,   O - ver the

hills and ev - ry - where.   Go,   tell it on the

moun - tain That Je - sus Christ___ is born.

125   The Trees of the Field

STEFFI GEISER RUBIN
Based on Isaiah 55:12

STUART DAUERMANN

You shall go out with joy ___ and be led forth with peace. ___ The moun-tains and the hills will break forth be - fore you; There'll be shouts of joy, ___ and all the trees of the field will clap, will clap their hands.

126 Every Day with Jesus

ROBERT C. LOVELESS

WENDELL P. LOVELESS

Ev - 'ry day with Je - sus Is sweet-er than the day be - fore;

Ev - 'ry day with Je - sus, I love Him more and more.

Je - sus saves and keeps me, And He's the One I'm wait-ing for.

Ev - 'ry day with Je - sus Is sweet-er than the day be - fore.

127 It Is Finished

P. N. and S. W. B.

PHIL NAISH and SCOTT WESLEY BROWN

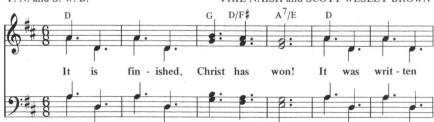

It is fin - ished, Christ has won! It was writ - ten

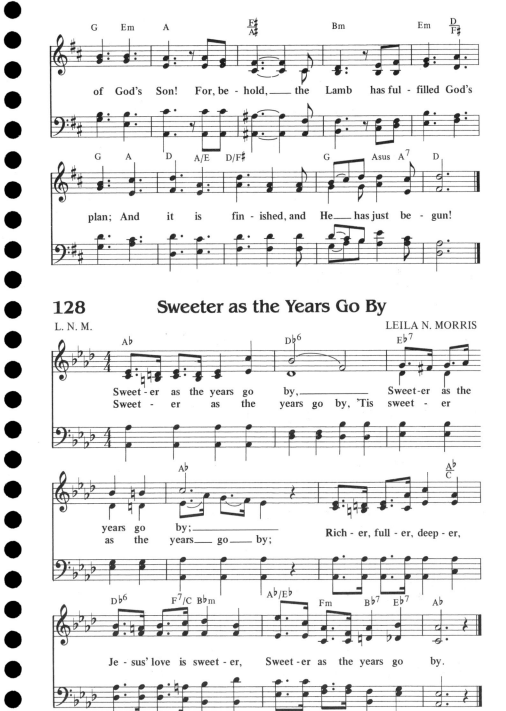

of God's Son! For, be - hold,___ the Lamb has ful - filled God's

plan; And it is fin - ished, and He___ has just be - gun!

128   Sweeter as the Years Go By

L. N. M.

LEILA N. MORRIS

Sweet - er as the years go by,___ Sweet-er as the
Sweet - er as the years go by, 'Tis sweet - er

years go by;___ Rich - er, full - er, deep - er,
as the years___ go ___ by;

Je - sus' love is sweet - er, Sweet-er as the years go by.

129 Something Beautiful

GLORIA GAITHER

WILLIAM J. GAITHER

Some-thing beau-it-ful, some-thing good; All my con-fu-sion He un-der-stood. All I had to of-fer Him was bro-ken-ness and strife, But He made some-thing beau-ti-ful of my life.

130   I've Got Peace like a River

Spiritual

Spiritual

Arr. by Lyndell Leatherman

1. I've got peace like a riv-er, I've got peace like a
2. I've got love like an o-cean, I've got love like an
3. I've got joy like a foun-tain, I've got joy like a

riv-er, I've got peace like a riv-er in my soul.
o-cean, I've got love like an o-cean in my soul.
foun-tain, I've got joy like a foun-tain in my soul.

I've got peace like a riv-er, I've got peace like a
I've got love like an o-cean, I've got love like an
I've got joy like a foun-tain, I've got joy like a

riv-er, I've got peace like a riv-er in my soul.
o-cean, I've got love like an o-cean in my soul.
foun-tain, I've got joy like a foun-tain in my soul.

131 Alive unto God

G. M.

GARY MOORE

A-live un-to God am I, ___ and hap-py and free. I'm fol-low-ing
Christ, the King; new pur-pose I see. Com - mit-ted to this ho-ly
way, My plea-sure to do His will. A-live un-to God am I, ___
___ and will-ing to go To those who are lost in sin ___ and wait-ing to
know, to know That life can be lived a - new when you're a - live un-to God!

Come a - live un - to God! Christ a - lone is a - ble to set you free.___

132   **Christ for Me!**

A. B.   ALEX BURNS

Christ   for   me,   Yes, it's   Christ   for

me!   He's   my   Sav - ior,   my   Lord   and   King—

I'm   so   hap - py I   shout   and   sing!   Ev - 'ry   day   as I

go   my   way It   is   Christ   for   me!_____

"Test Me now in this," says the Lord of hosts, "if I will not open for you the windows of heaven, and pour out for you a blessing until it overflows" (Malachi 3:10).

133 The Windows of Heaven Are Open

Unknown

Unknown

The win-dows of heav-en are o-pen,___ The bless-ings are fall-ing to-night;___ There's joy, joy, joy in my soul Since Je-sus made ev-'ry-thing right.___ I gave Him my old, tat-tered gar-ments;___ He gave me a robe of pure white.___ I'm feast-ing on hon-ey from Ca-naan,___ And that's why I'm hap-py to-night.___

134 Things Are Different Now

S. W. G.

STANTON W. GAVITT

Things are dif-f'rent now, Some-thing hap-pened to me When I gave my heart to Je - sus. Things are dif - f'rent
(D.S.) Things are dif - f'rent

now— I was chang'd, it must be, When I gave my heart to
now, Some-thing hap - pened that day When I gave my heart to

Him.————— Things I loved be - fore have passed a -
Him.—————

way, Things I love far more have come to stay;

135 When I Met the Man of Calvary

G. M.

GARY MOORE

When I met the Man of Cal - va - ry, He gave life to me!
Now a-bun-dant life He gives to me, New joy ev - 'ry day!

Then I let the Spir-it have con-trol, His on - ly to be.
From the fol - ly of this world I'm free, For Christ is the Way.

I've sur-ren-dered all my tal - ents now; To Him I have made this vow:

His guid-ance I will al - low; My-self to de - ny!

Turn back from my Lord? Well, why? A - live un - to God am I!

In the cen-ter of His will I'll stay   Till Je-sus I see!

136   Life Is a Symphony

B. B. B.

BEATRICE BUSH BIXLER

Life is a sym-pho-ny   Since the Man of Gal-i-lee

Changed my dis-cords in-to song,   Made life sweet the whole day long.

Life is a sym-pho-ny,   Praise the Man of Gal-i-lee!

No more a stran-ger—He is the ar-ran-ger of my sym-pho-ny!

137

I Can, I Will, I Do Believe
(with Take Me as I Am)

Trad. and ELIZA H. HAMILTON

Trad. and J. H. STOCKTON
Arr. by Lyndell Leatherman

I can, I will, I do be-lieve;— I can, I will, I do be-lieve;— I can, I will, I do be-lieve— That Je-sus saves me now.— He takes me as— I am;— He takes me as— I am.— He brings His free sal-va-tion to me, And takes me as I am.—

138 Glory Hallelujah!

LELAND GREEN and N. E. B.

NORAH E. BURNE

Glo - ry, hal - le - lu - jah! Christ has set me

free; Glo - ry, hal - le - lu - jah! A

new life now I see. My sins are all for-giv'n, I'm

on my way to heav'n To live e - ter - nal - ly.

Glo - ry, hal - le - lu - jah! He's com - ing soon for me!

Discipleship

139   ## People Need the Lord

G. N. and P. McH.

GREG NELSON and PHILL McHUGH

Peo-ple need the Lord, peo-ple need the Lord.

At the end of bro-ken dreams___ He's the o-pen door.___
When___ will we

re-al-ize___ that peo-ple need the Lord.___

140 My Hands Belong to You

A. W. and F. H.

ANE WEBER and FRANK HERNANDEZ

My hands be-long
voice be-longs to You, Lord; My
heart be-longs

hands be-long
voice be-longs to You. I lift them it
heart be-longs it

up to You, Lord, And sing hal-le-

lu-jah. I lift them it up to You,
it

Lord, And sing hal-le-lu-jah.

141 My Desire

L. P.

LILLIAN PLANKENHORN

My de - sire——— to be like Je - sus; My de - sire———
——— to be like Him!——— His Spir - it fill me,——— His love o'er -
whelm me;——— In deed and word——— to be like Him!———

142 I'll Be True, Precious Jesus

Unknown

Unknown

1. I'll be true, pre-cious Je - sus, I'll be true. I'll be true, pre-cious
2. I'll go through, pre-cious Je - sus, I'll go through. I'll go through, pre-cious

143 **More than Conquerors**

B. G. and J. G.

BILL and JANNY GREIN

Je-sus, I'll be true.
Je-sus, I'll go through. There's a race to be run; There's a
vic-t'ry to be won. Ev-'ry hour,— by Thy pow-er, I'll be true.

We've been made more than con-quer-ors, o-ver-
com-ers in this life. We've been made vic-
to-ri-ous through the blood of Je-sus Christ.

144 Whatever It Takes

L. W. and MARIETTA WOLFE

LANNY WOLFE

my will to break, That's what I'll be will-ing to do.___

145   We Are His Hands

M. G.

MARK GERSMEHL

We are His hands,___ we are His feet;___ We are His

peo - ple, chil - dren of the Lord.___ We

share the hope,___ we share the dream;___ Be - liev - ers in

Je - sus, chil - dren of the King!___

146 Jesus Is Lord

ED SEABOUGH
Based on Rom. 10:10, Phil. 2:9-11

OT SKILLINGS

1. With my heart I be-lieve, Je-sus Christ is___ Lord; And that
(2) lips I con-fess, Je-sus Christ is___ Lord; And I,

Je-sus rose a-gain, Je-sus Christ is Lord. 2. With my
too, shall live a-gain, Je-sus Christ is Lord.

Je-sus is Lord, Lord of my life; Je-sus is

Lord, Lord of my life. Je-sus is Lord,

Lord of my life; Je-sus is Lord.___

. . . at the name of Jesus every knee should bow . . . and every tongue should confess that Jesus Christ is Lord, to the glory of God the Father (Philippians 2:10-11).

147   Jesus Is Lord of All

W. J. and GLORIA GAITHER   WILLIAM J. GAITHER

1. All my to-mor-rows, all my past; Je-sus is Lord of all. — I've quit my strug-gles, con-tent-ment at last;
2. All of my con-flicts, all my thoughts; Je-sus is Lord of all. — His love wins the bat-tles I could not have fought;
3. All of my long-ings, all my dreams; Je-sus is Lord of all. — All of my fail-ures His pow-er re-deems;

Refrain

Je-sus is Lord of all. — King of kings, Lord of lords; Je-sus is Lord of all. — All my pos-sess-ions and all my life; Je-sus is Lord of all. —

148 Seek Ye First

K. L.

KAREN LAFFERTY

1. Seek ye first the kingdom of God And His
2. Ask and it shall be given unto you; Seek and

right - eous - ness; And all these things shall be
you shall find; Knock and it shall be

add-ed un-to you. Hal-le - lu, Hal-le - lu - jah.
o-pened un-to you. Hal-le - lu, Hal-le - lu - jah.

Let your light shine before men in such a way that they may see your good works, and glorify your Father who is in heaven (Matthew 5:16).

149 Lord, Be Glorified

B. K.

BOB KILPATRICK

Moderato

In my life church, Lord, be glor-i-fied, be glor-i-fied.
your

In my life Lord, be glor-i-fied _____ to - day.
your church,

150   Is There Anything I Can Do for You?

D. R. and D. H.

DOTTIE RAMBO and DAVID HUNTSINGER

1. Is there an-y-thing__I can do for You? An-y-thing__I can do? For__
2. Is there an-y-thing__I can be for You? An-y-thing__I can be? For__
3. Is there an-y-where_I can go for You? An-y-where_I can go? For -

all the things You've done for me, Is there an-y-thing__I can__ do?
all the things You've been to me, Is there an-y-thing__I can__ be? I'm
sak-ing all to fol-low Thee, Is there an-y-where_I can__ go?

will-ing to be used, dear Lord, What-e'er the price may be. So if there's

an-y-thing _____ I can { do / be / go } for You, Just make it known to me.
(an-y-where)

How firm a foundation, ye saints of the Lord,
Is laid for your faith in His excellent Word!

151 Goin' to Build My Life

D. A.

DICK ANTHONY

1. Goin' to build my life on the Word of God; Goin' to turn my feet in the nar-row way that the saints have trod. Goin' to set my heart on things a-bove, And tell the world that I am full of the Sav-ior's love.

2. Goin' to tune my ears to the Spir-it's voice; Goin' to pray that He will lead my life in His ho-ly choice. Goin' to use my hands the way He plans, And dai-ly try my best to do what the Lord com-mands.

3. Goin' to tell my friends 'bout the Je-sus way; Goin' to let them know that He can change the night to day. Goin' to use my time in things di-vine, And show the world that I am His and He is mine.

We love, because He first loved us (1 John 4:19).

152   I Will Serve Thee

W. J. and GLORIA GAITHER   WILLIAM J. GAITHER

I will serve Thee be - cause I love Thee; You have
I was noth - ing be - fore You found me; You have

giv - en life to me.
giv - en life to me.

Heart - aches, bro - ken piec - es, Ru - ined

lives are why You died on Cal - vary. Your touch was what I

longed for; You have giv - en life to me.

153 With Eternity's Values in View

A. S.

AL SMITH

With e - ter - ni - ty's val - ues in view, Lord; With e - ter - ni - ty's
val - ues in view—— May I do each day's work for
Je - sus With e - ter - ni - ty's val - ues in view.——

154 This Is My Prayer

D. H.

DOUG HOLCK

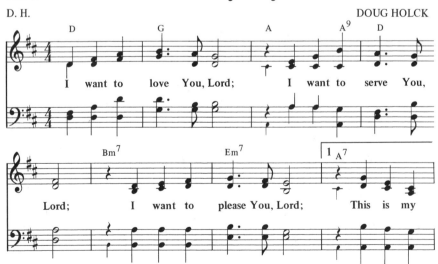

I want to love You, Lord; I want to serve You,
Lord; I want to please You, Lord; This is my

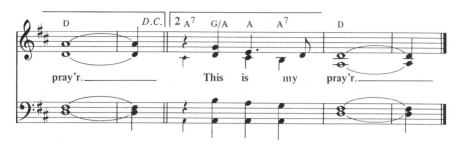

pray'r. _____ This is my pray'r. _____

155   We Will Stand

RUSS TAFF and TORI TAFF   JAMES HOLLIHAN

You're my broth-er, you're my sis - er, so take me by the hand;

To - geth-er we will work un-til He comes. _____

_____ There's no foe that can de-feat _____ us when we're walk-ing side by side; _____

_____ As long as there is love, _____ we will stand. _____

156   Now Walk with God

O. S.

OTIS SKILLINGS

On God's ho-ly Word I chal-lenge you— To give to the Lord your life a-new.
— My friend, make your choice; He waits for you,— For this is the mo-ment of
truth.— Now walk with God and He will be your dear-est Friend,—
— Wher-e'er you go, in ev-'ry-thing you do.
And may your life re - flect His love to ev - 'ry-one.

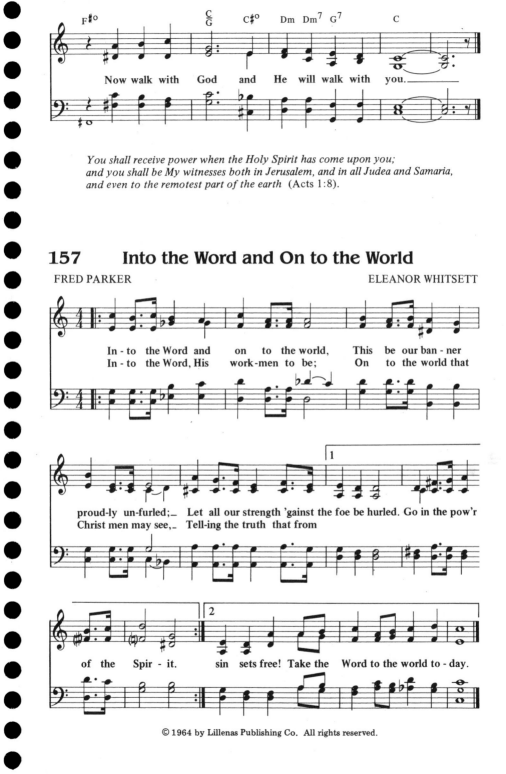

Now walk with God and He will walk with you._____

You shall receive power when the Holy Spirit has come upon you;
and you shall be My witnesses both in Jerusalem, and in all Judea and Samaria,
and even to the remotest part of the earth (Acts 1:8).

157 Into the Word and On to the World

FRED PARKER   ELEANOR WHITSETT

In - to the Word and on to the world, This be our ban - ner
In - to the Word, His work-men to be; On to the world that

proud-ly un-furled;_ Let all our strength 'gainst the foe be hurled. Go in the pow'r
Christ men may see,_ Tell-ing the truth that from

of the Spir - it. sin sets free! Take the Word to the world to - day.

158   I Love You with the Love of the Lord

J. G.

JAMES GILBERT

I ___ love you with the love ___ of the Lord, ___

Yes, I love you with the love ___ of the Lord. ___

I can see in you the ___ glo-ry of my King,

And I love you with the love ___ of the Lord. ___

159   All Power Is Given unto Me

Adapted from Matthew 28:18, 20

JAMES McGRANAHAN

All pow'r is giv-en un-to Me, All pow'r is giv-en un-to Me;

Go ye in-to all the world and preach the gos-pel And, lo, I am with you al - way.

160   He's Still Workin' on Me

J. H.

JOEL HEMPHILL

He's still work-in' on me to make me what I ought to be;

It took Him just a week to make the moon and stars, The

sun and the earth and Ju - pi - ter and Mars. How lov - ing and

pa - tient He must be! He's still work-in' on me!_____

161 Spirit of the Living God

DANIEL IVERSON
Arr. by Tom Fettke

D. I.

Spir - it of the liv - ing God, Fall fresh on me.

Spir - it of the liv - ing God, Fall fresh on me.

Melt me, mold me, fill me, use me.

Spir - it of the liv - ing God, Fall fresh on me.

162 Lord, Lay Some Soul upon My Heart

LEON TUCKER

IRA D. SANKEY

Lord, lay some soul up - on my heart And love that soul through me;—

And may I glad - ly do my part To win that soul for Thee.

163   We Shall Overcome

J. H.

JACK HAYFORD

We shall o - ver - come,   we shall o - ver -

come By the Word of God and the blood of the Lamb and the

name of our Lord Je-sus Christ.   name of our Lord Je-sus Christ;

By the Word and the blood and the name of our Lord Je-sus Christ.

2 Corinthians 3:18

Unknown

per - fect in me— The love of God shown to the world._____

165 Let the Beauty of Jesus Be Seen in Me

ALBERT ORSBORN   TOM JONES

Let   the   beau-ty of Je - sus be   seen   in   me—

All   His   won-der-ful pas-sion and   pu - ri - ty!

O   Thou Spir-it di - vine, All   my   na-ture re - fine

Till   the   beau-ty of Je - sus be   seen   in   me.

166 We Are the Body of the Lord

LINDA LEE JOHNSON

TOM FETTKE

1. We are the bod-y of the Lord;___ We are the
2. We are the tem-ple of the Lord;___ We are the

bod-y of the Lord.___ U - nit - ed in Christ and
tem-ple of the Lord.___ U - nit - ed in love and

work - ing to-geth-er, We are the bod-y of the Lord.
grow - ing to-geth-er, We are the tem-ple of the Lord.

167 Whisper a Prayer

Arr. by Hugh C. Benner

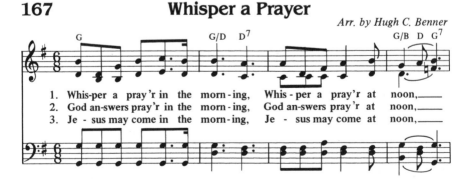

1. Whis-per a pray'r in the morn-ing, Whis-per a pray'r at noon,___
2. God an-swers pray'r in the morn-ing, God an-swers pray'r at noon,___
3. Je - sus may come in the morn-ing, Je - sus may come at noon,___

Whis-per a pray'r in the eve-ning To keep—your heart in tune.___
God an-swers pray'r in the eve-ning; He'll keep—your heart in tune.___
Je-sus may come in the eve-ning; So keep—your heart in tune.___

168   More of You

GLORIA GAITHER   WILLIAM J. GAITHER and GARY S. PAXTON

More of You,___ more of You;___ I've had
all but what I need— just more of You.___ Of things I've
had my fill,___ and yet I hun-ger still.___ Emp-ty and
bare, Lord, hear my prayer for more___ of You.___

169 Not My Will

Unknown

Unknown
Arr. by Lyndell Leatherman

Not my will ___ but Thine be done, ___ But let the
full - ness of the Son Rule with - in ___ this life that
I ___ have of - fered Thee. ___ Un - til ev - 'ry-thing I
do ___ Be-comes the thing ___ that pleas-es You. Ab - ba,
Fa - ther, I would be ___ a Son in - deed. ___

170   Clean Hands, Pure Heart

J. S. and M. G.

JOHN SLICK and MARK GERSMEHL

Clean hands, a pure heart con-se-crat-ed to You; _____ O - pen, bro - ken in__ all I say__ and __ do. Oh, dear_ Lord, _____ give me clean hands, a pure heart shin - ing __ for You. _____

171

Into My Heart

H. D. C.

HARRY D. CLARK

In - to my heart, in - to my heart, Come in - to my heart, Lord Je - sus. Come in to - day, come in to stay— Come in - to my heart, Lord Je - sus.

172

Above All Else

J. W. P.

JOHN W. PETERSON

A - bove all else_____ the world needs Je-sus,____ As shad - ows fall_____
He is the best____ of earth's pos - ses - sions; A - bove all else_____
(D.C.) A - bove all else_____ the world needs Je - sus; A - bove all else_____

173   **His**

DON COWLEY

VIRGINIA POPLIN COWLEY

and hopes grow dim.
the world needs Him.
the world needs Him. For He can lift a soul from dark de-spair,

Save from sin and an-swer pray'r. There is not an-oth-er friend like Je-sus!

His is my soul, re - deemed from all sin. His is my heart, pur - i - fied with - in. His is my life, trans-formed from a - bove; His my whole be - ing— an of - f'ring of love!

174   **O to Be like Thee**

THOMAS O. CHISHOLM   WILLIAM J. KIRKPATRICK

Oh, to be like Thee! Oh, to be like Thee, bless-ed Re-
deem - er, pure as Thou art! Come in Thy sweet - ness,
come in Thy full - ness; Stamp Thine own im - age deep on my heart.

175   **I Have Decided to Follow Jesus**

Unknown   Indian Folk Melody

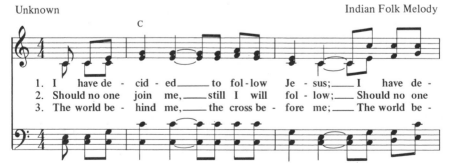

1. I   have de - cid - ed____ to fol-low   Je - sus;____ I   have de -
2. Should no one   join me,____still I will   fol - low;____ Should no one
3. The world be - hind me,____ the cross be - fore me;____ The world be -

cid - ed_____ to fol - low Je - sus;_____ I have de - cid - ed_____ to
join me,_____ still I will fol - low; Should no one join me,_____ still
hind me,_____ the cross be - fore me;_____ The world be - hind me,_____ the

fol - low Je - sus._____
I will fol - low._____ No turn-ing back,_____ no turn-ing back!
cross be - fore me._____

176   To Be like Jesus

JOHN GOWANS   JOHN LARSSON

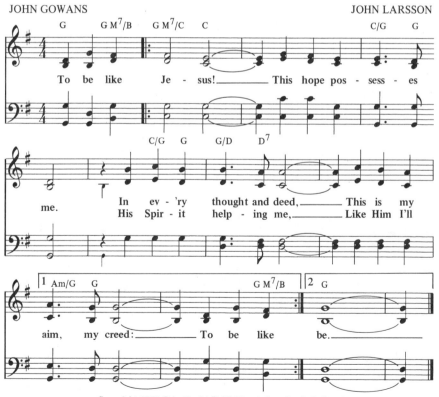

To be like Je - sus!_____ This hope pos - sess - es
me.

In ev - 'ry thought and deed,_____ This is my
His Spir - it help - ing me,_____ Like Him I'll

aim, my creed:_____ To be like
be._____

177

Let Me Burn Out for Thee

B. F. H.

BESSIE F. HATCHER

Let me burn out for Thee, dear Lord; Burn and wear out for Thee.

Don't let me rust, or my life be A fail - ure, my God, to

Thee. Thee___ (to Thee). Use me and all I have, dear Lord, And

get me so close to Thee_____ That I feel the throb of the

great heart of God, Un - til I burn out for Thee.____

178 Make Me a Servant

K. W.

KELLY WILLARD

Make me a ser-vant, hum-ble and meek;

Lord, let me lift up those who are weak;

And may the pray'r of my heart al-ways be:

Make me a ser-vant, make me a ser-vant,

Make me a ser-vant to-day.

179

God Calls Us

LINDA REBUCK

TOM FETTKE

1. Be - cause so man - y need to know, It's up to
2. Be - cause so man - y need to see That God a -
3. Be - cause so man - y need to hear, I want to

you___ and me to go. Be - cause so man - y
lone___ can make them free. Be - cause so man - y
be___ a vol - un - teer. Be - cause so man - y

need___ to know,
need___ to see, God calls___ us, God calls us.
need___ to hear,

180

Just a Closer Walk with Thee

Unknown

Traditional Folk Song

I am weak but Thou art strong;___ Je - sus, keep me from all wrong.___
Just a clos-er walk with Thee;___ Grant it, Je - sus, is my plea.___

181   **Pray for Me**

D. W.

DAN WHITTEMORE

Pray for me,   I'll pray for you

That we be filled with the knowl-edge of His will.

In all wis-dom and spir-it-ual un-der-stand-

ing, that we might walk in a way that pleas-es God.

182   Lord, I Want to Be a Christian

Negro Spiritual

1. Lord, I want to be a Chris-tian In my heart, in my heart._____
2. Lord, I want to be more lov-ing In my heart, in my heart._____
3. Lord, I want to be more ho-ly In my heart, in my heart._____
4. Lord, I want to be like Je-sus In my heart, in my heart._____

Lord, I want to be a Chris-tian In my heart._____
Lord, I want to be more lov-ing In my heart._____
Lord, I want to be more ho-ly In my heart._____
Lord, I want to be like Je-sus In my heart._____

Refrain

In my heart,_____ in my heart;_____
(in my heart,) (in my heart;)

183   To Be like Jesus

Unknown

Unknown   *Arr. by Lyndell Leatherman*

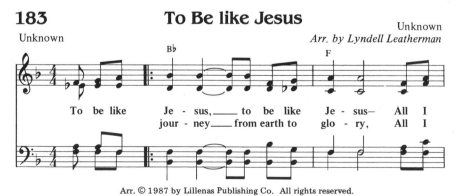

To be like Je - sus,_____ to be like Je - sus— All I
jour - ney_____ from earth to glo - ry, All I

ask,___ to be like Him. All thro' life's

ask,___ to be like Him.___

184   Lead Me to Some Soul Today

WILL H. HOUGHTON   WENDELL P. LOVELESS

Lead me to some soul to-day; Oh, teach me, Lord, just what to say;___

Friends of mine are lost in sin And can-not find their way.

Few there are___who seem to care, And few there are___who pray.___

who pray.

Melt my heart and fill my life, Give me___one soul to - day.

185 Your Love Compels Me

D. H.

DOUG HOLCK

Your love com-pels me, Lord, to give as You would give,

To speak as You would speak, to live as You would live.

Your love com-pels me, Lord, to see as You would see,

To serve as You would serve, to be what You would be.

186 We'll Work Till Jesus Comes

ELIZABETH MILLS

WILLIAM MILLER

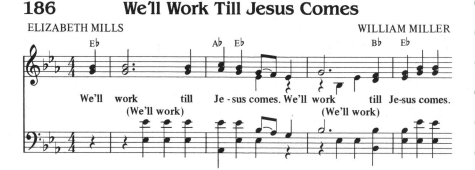

We'll work till Je-sus comes. We'll work till Je-sus comes.
(We'll work)   (We'll work)

We'll work till Je - sus comes, And we'll be gath-ered home.
(We'll work)

187   To Be Used of God

A. M.

AUDREY MIEIR

To be used of God to speak, to sing, to
To be used of God to show some-one the

pray. _____ way. _____ Oh,

how I long to feel the touch of His con-sum-ing fire.

To be used of God _____ is my de - sire. _____

188   That the World May Know

S. C.

SUE CAUDILL

I want the world to know_____ that Je - sus loves them so.__

_____ I want His life and cleans-ing pow'r to flow through me.__

_____ If we will join our hands_____ and do as He com-mands,_____

_____ Then to - geth - er we'll reach out an arm of love._____

_____ I want the world to see_____ Je - sus in you and me,__

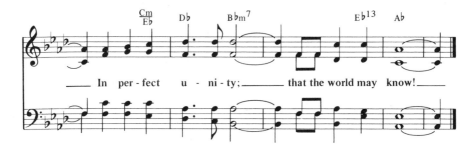

In per - fect u - ni - ty; ____ that the world may know! ____

189   Teach Me, Lord

LINDA REBUCK   TOM FETTKE

Teach me, Lord; teach me, Lord; Teach me to

do ____ Your will. ____ trust and o -

bey. ____ I will lis - ten as You speak in Your still, small

voice; As You teach me each day ____ to make the right choice. ____

190 Always Remember

A. C.

ANDRAÉ CROUCH

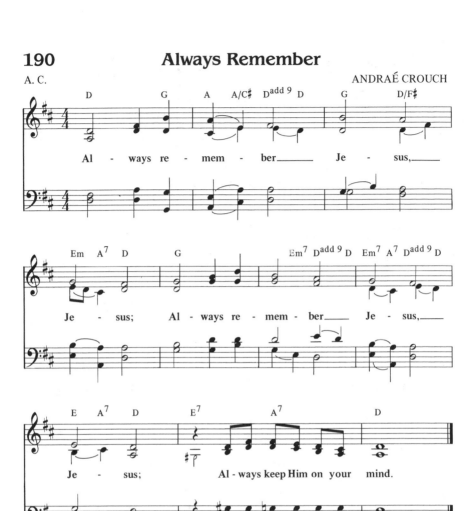

Al - ways re - mem - ber____ Je - sus,____
Je - sus; Al - ways re - mem - ber____ Je - sus,____
Je - sus; Al - ways keep Him on your mind.

191 Nothing Between

C. A. T.

C. A. TINDLEY

Noth-ing be - tween my soul and the Sav - ior, So that His

bless - ed face may be seen. Noth - ing pre - vent-ing the

least of His fa - vor. Keep the way clear: let noth-ing be - tween.

192   Not My Will, but Thine

H. C. B.

HUGH C. BENNER

Not my will, but Thine; not my will, but Thine; Not my will but

Thy will be done, Lord, in me. May Thy Spir - it di - vine fill this

be - ing of mine. Not my will, but Thy will be done, Lord, in me.

193

So Send I You

O. S.

OTIS SKILLINGS

The har - vest is great, but the work-ers are few; so send I you. I have or-dained and— cho - sen— you; so send I— you.— You are my wit - ness at home and a - broad; so send I you.— Preach-ing with pow-er the king - dom of God; so— send I you. Un - to the ut - ter-most part of the earth, Pro-claim-ing the mes-sage 'til

all men have heard. As the Fa-ther hath sent_me, so_send I you.

194 Share His Love

W. J. R.

WILLIAM J. REYNOLDS

Share His love by tell-ing what the Lord has done for you; Share His love by shar-ing of your faith;____ ____ And show the world that Je-sus Christ is real to you Ev-'ry mo-ment,____ ev-'ry day.____

195   # Every Moment of Every Day

N. J. C.

NORMAN J. CLAYTON

196 The Greatest Thing

M. P.

MARK PENDERGRASS

The great-est thing in all my life is lov - ing You; The
serv - ing knowing

great-est thing in all my life is lov - ing You.
serv - ing knowing

I want to love You more, I want to love You more.
serve serve know know

The great-est thing in all my life is lov - ing You.
serv - ing knowing

Be imitators of God, as beloved children; and walk in love,
just as Christ also loved you (Ephesians 5:1-2).

197 I Must Have Jesus

Traditional

Traditional
Arr. by Lyndell Leatherman

1. I must have Je - sus in my whole life; I must have
2. I have Christ Je - sus in my whole life; I have Christ

Je - sus in my life. In my walk-ing, in my talk-ing, in my
Je - sus in my life. In my walk-ing, in my talk-ing, in my

sleep-ing, in my wak -ing; I must have Je - sus in my life.
sleep-ing, in my wak -ing; I have Christ Je - sus in my life.

198 I Live by Faith

Adapted from Gal. 2:20

C. C. DUNBAR

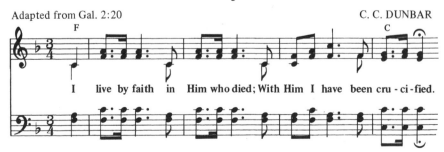

I live by faith in Him who died; With Him I have been cru - ci -fied.

I live and yet it is not I, But Christ who lives in me.

199   Let Them Know

LANNY and MARIETTA WOLFE   LANNY WOLFE

Let them know, let them know;___ Tell them Je - sus loves them

so; Loves them so much that to Cal-va-ry He would go.___

___ Let them know, let them know___ That they, too, can

go To live for - ev - er - more with Je - sus. Let them know,___ let them know.

200

Little by Little

Unknown

Unknown
Arr. by Lyndell Leatherman

Lit - tle by lit - tle He's chang - ing me, Line af - ter line____ un - til I can see, Pre - cept on pre - cept un - til I am free; Je - sus is chang - ing me.____

201

I Know the Lord Will Make a Way

Unknown

Unknown
Arr. by Haldor Lillenas

1. I know the Lord will make a way for_ me;____ I know the Lord
2. I want the Lord to have His way with_ me;____ I want the Lord

will make a way for me.___ If I live a ho-ly life, Shun the
to have His way with me.___ Tho' the need be great or small, I would

wrong and do the right, I know the Lord will make a way for me.___
yield to Him my all, I want the Lord to have His way with me.___

202   Keep Me True

Unknown

Unknown

Arr. by Lyndell Leatherman

Keep me true, Lord Je-sus, keep me true. Keep me true, Lord

Je-sus, keep me true. There's a race that must be run; There's a vic't'ry to be

won. Ev-'ry hour,___ by Thy pow'r,___ keep me true.

203   **Be Still and Know**

Unknown
Arr. by Lyndell Leatherman

Adapted

1. Be still and know that I am God. Be still and know that I am God. Be still and know that I am God.
2. I am the Lord that heal-eth thee. I am the Lord that heal-eth thee. I am the Lord that heal-eth thee.
3. In Thee, O Lord, I put my trust. In Thee, O Lord, I put my trust. In Thee, O Lord, I put my trust.

204   In His Time

Adapted by D. B.

DIANE BALL

1. In His time (in His time), in His time (in His time),
2. In Your time (in Your time), in Your time (in Your time),

He makes all things beau-ti - ful in His time (in His time).
You make all things beau-ti - ful in Your time (in Your time).

Lord, please show me ev - 'ry day as You're teach-ing me Your way,
Lord, my life to You I bring; May each song I have to sing

That You do just what You say in Your time (in Your time).
Be to You a love - ly thing in Your time (in Your time).

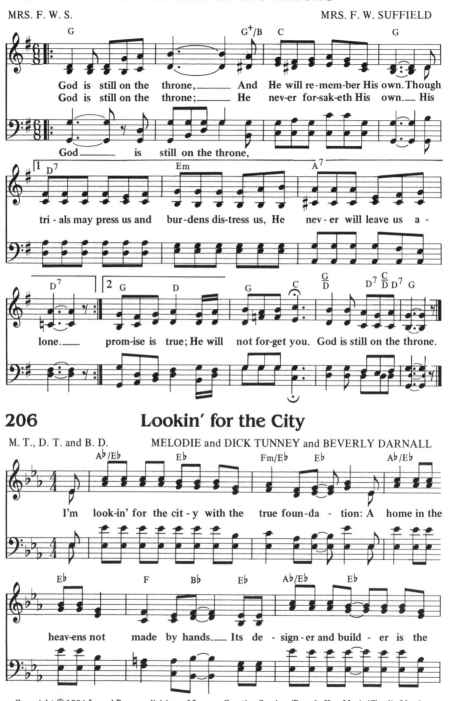

205   God Is Still on the Throne

MRS. F. W. S.

MRS. F. W. SUFFIELD

God is still on the throne,_____ And He will re-mem-ber His own. Though
God is still on the throne;_____ He nev-er for-sak-eth His own.__ His

God_____ is still on the throne,

tri - als may press us and bur-dens dis-tress us, He nev - er will leave us a -

lone.____ prom-ise is true; He will not for-get you. God is still on the throne.

206   Lookin' for the City

M. T., D. T. and B. D.

MELODIE and DICK TUNNEY and BEVERLY DARNALL

I'm look-in' for the cit - y with the true foun-da - tion: A home in the

heav-ens not made by hands.__ Its de - sign - er and build - er is the

Lord of the a - ges; He pre - pared it for me___ be - fore the world be - gan.___

207   God Can Do Anything but Fail

I. F. S.

IRA F. STANPHILL

God can do an - y - thing, an - y - thing, an - y - thing; God can
He can save, He can keep, He can cleanse, and He will; God can

do an - y - thing but fail.___
do an - y - thing but fail.___ He's the Al - pha and O - me - ga, the be -

gin - ning and the end; He's the fair - est of ten thou - sand to my soul.___ God can

do an - y - thing, an - y - thing, an - y - thing; God can do an - y - thing but fail.

208

I Shall Not Be Moved

Traditional

Traditional
Arr. by Lyndell Leatherman

1. Glo-ry, hal-le-lu - jah! An-chored in Je-
2. In His love a-bid - ing, I shall not be moved. And in Him con-
3. Tho' the tem-pest rag - es, On the Rock of

Chorus: I____ shall____ not be, I shall not be moved. I____ shall____

ho - vah,
fid - ing, I shall not be moved. Just like a tree that's plant-ed by the
A - ges,
not be,

I shall not be moved.

wa - ters,____ I shall not, shall not be moved.

I shall not be moved.

209

These Times—God Is Able

R. L.
Verses 2 and 3 by MOSIE LISTER

RON LUSH

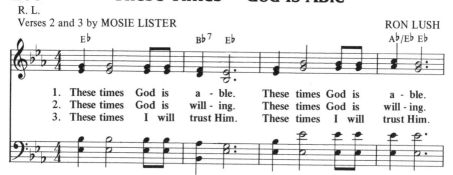

1. These times God is a - ble. These times God is a - ble.
2. These times God is will - ing. These times God is will - ing.
3. These times I will trust Him. These times I will trust Him.

These times God is a - ble to car - ry you through.
These times God is will - ing to car - ry you through.
These times I will trust Him; He'll car - ry me through.

210   Peace in the Midst of the Storm

S. R. A.

STEPHEN R. ADAMS

There is peace in the midst of my storm - tossed

life; Oh, there's an An-chor, there's a Rock to cast my faith up-on.___

___ Je - sus rides in my ves-sel___ so I'll fear no a-

larm; He gives me peace in the midst of my storm!___

211

Listen

O. S.

OTIS SKILLINGS

Lis-ten;___ ev-'ry-bod-y lis-ten, lis-ten.___ Ev-'ry-bod-y lis-ten,

lis-ten.___ 1. Ev-'ry-bod-y lis-ten. Come to Christ to-day.
2. Ev-'ry-bod-y lis-ten. He will hear you

pray.___ Lis-ten;___ ev-'ry-bod-y lis-ten, lis-ten.___

Ev-'ry-bod-y lis-ten, lis-ten.___ Ev-'ry-bod-y lis-ten. Come to Christ to-

day. He will hear you pray. Come to Christ to-day.

212 He's Able

P. E. P.

PAUL E. PAINO
Arr. by Lyndell Leatherman

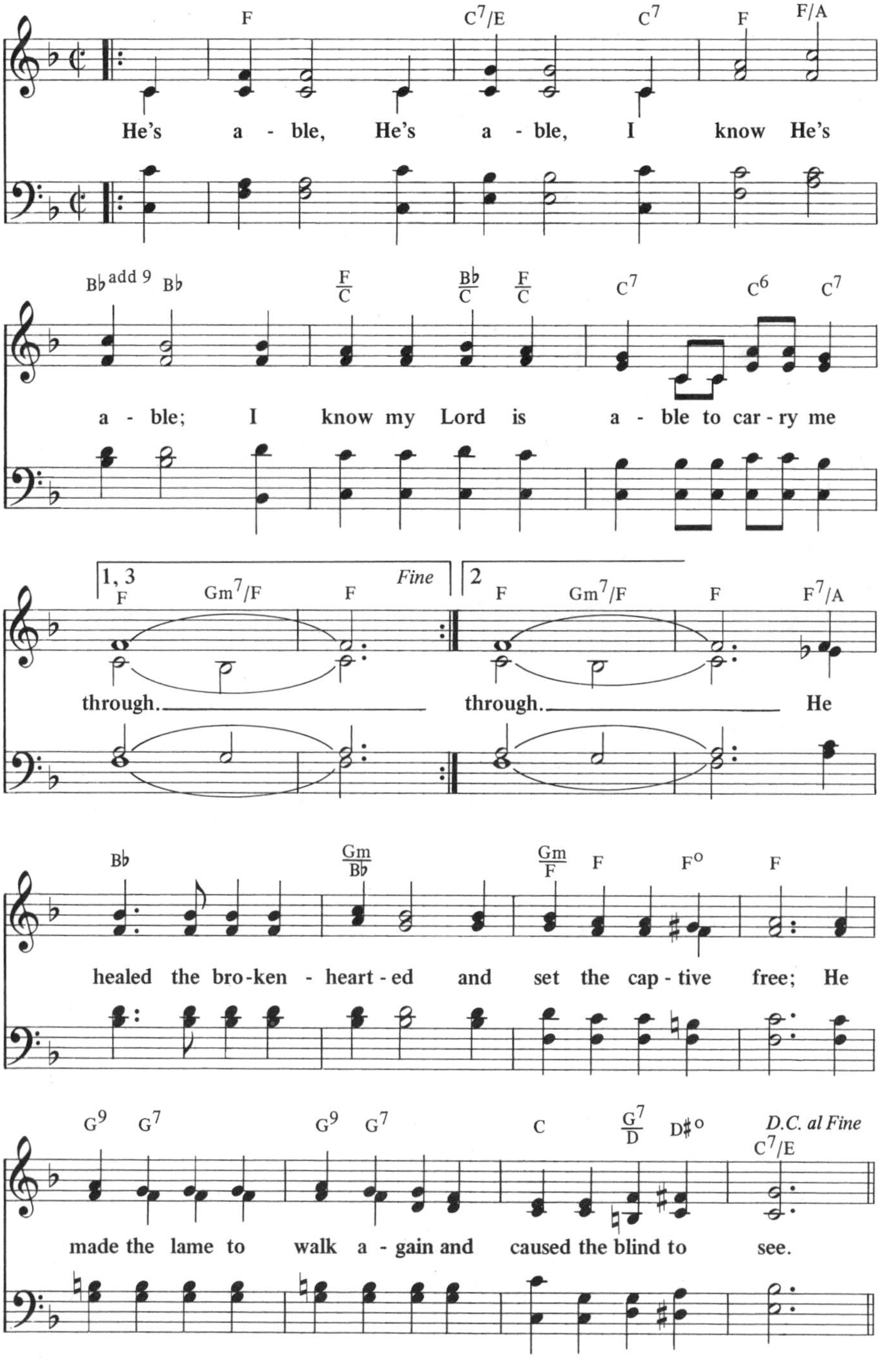

F C7/E C7 F F/A
He's a - ble, He's a - ble, I know He's
Bb add 9 Bb F/C Bb/C F/C C7 C6 C7
a - ble; I know my Lord is a - ble to car - ry me
1, 3
F Gm7/F F
Fine
2
F Gm7/F F F7/A
through. through. He
Bb Gm/Bb Gm/F F F° F
healed the bro - ken - heart - ed and set the cap - tive free; He
G9 G7 G9 G7 C G7/D D#°
D.C. al Fine
C7/E
made the lame to walk a - gain and caused the blind to see.

213   **I Just Keep Trusting My Lord**

J. W. P.

JOHN W. PETERSON

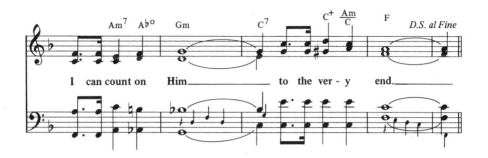

I can count on Him____ to the ver - y end.____

214 He's Got the Whole World in His Hands

Spiritual

1. He's got the whole____ world____ in His hands;__ He's got the
2. He's got the wind and rain____ in His hands;__ He's got the
3. He's got____ you and me____ in His hands;__ He's got____
4. He's got____ ev - 'ry - bod-y____ in His hands;__ He's got____

whole wide world____ in His hands;__ He's got the whole____ world
wind and rain____ in His hands;__ He's got the wind and rain____
you and me____ in His hands;__ He's got____ you and me____
ev - 'ry - bod-y____ in His hands;__ He's got____ ev - 'ry - bod-y____

in His hands.__ He's got the whole world in His hands.____
in His hands.__ He's got the whole world in His hands.____
in His hands.__ He's got the whole world in His hands.____
in His hands.__ He's got the whole world in His hands.____

215

No, Never Alone

Unknown   Unknown

No, nev-er a - lone;_____ No, nev-er a - lone._____

He prom-ised nev-er to leave me; He'll claim me for___ His

own.   leave me,   Nev - er to leave me a - lone.

216

My Lord Knows the Way

S. E. C.   SIDNEY E. COX

My Lord knows the way thro' the wil-der-ness; All I have to

do is fol - low.   fol - low. Strength for to - day is

mine all the way, And all I need for to - mor - row!

217   Kum-ba-yah

Traditional

African Melody
Arr. by Steve Reynolds

Ref. *Kum - ba - yah, my Lord,_____
1. Some - one's cry - ing, Lord;_____ Kum - ba - yah._____
2. Some - one's pray - ing, Lord;_____
3. Some - one's sing - ing, Lord;_____

Kum - ba - yah, my Lord,_____
Some-one's cry - ing, Lord;_____ Kum - ba - yah._____
Some-one's pray - ing, Lord;_____
Some-one's sing - ing, Lord;_____

Kum - ba - yah, my Lord,_____
Some-one's cry - ing, Lord;_____ Kum - ba - yah._____
Some-one's pray - ing, Lord;_____
Some-one's sing - ing, Lord;_____

_____ O Lord, _____ kum - ba - yah._____

*"Kum-ba-yah" can be replaced with the phrase, "Come by here."

If you have faith as a mustard seed, you shall say to this mountain, "Move from here to there," and it shall move; and nothing shall be impossible to you (Matthew 17:20).

218 Faith, Mighty Faith, the Promise Sees

CHARLES WESLEY

Unknown
Arr. by Lyndell Leatherman

219

Not by Might

Adapted from Zech. 4:6-7 by A. H.

ALMEDA HERRICK

"Not by might, ____ not by pow'r, ____ but by my

Spir - it," saith the Lord of Hosts. Lord. ____

This moun - tain shall be re - moved; ____ This

moun-tain ____ shall be re - moved, ____ This moun-tain shall be re -

moved ____ "By My Spir - it," saith the Lord.

220
All Your Anxiety

E. H. J.

EDWARD HENRY JOY

All your anx - i - e - ty, all your care, Bring to the
mer - cy seat— leave it there. Nev - er a bur - den He
can - not bear,_____ Nev - er a friend like Je - sus!

221
Through It All

A. C.

ANDRAÉ CROUCH

Through it all,_____ through it all,_____ Oh, I've

222   **Listen, Jesus Is Calling You**

Traditional

Arr. by Lyndell Leatherman

Traditional

Lis - ten, Je - sus is call - ing you, Call - ing
you, call - ing you. Come to Him, He will your
heart re - new; Call - ing, call - ing you.

223 With God Nothing Is Impossible

D. H.

DOUG HOLCK

With God there is noth-ing im - pos - si - ble.

With God there is noth-ing that He can-not do.

With God there is noth-ing im - pos - si - ble;

There's noth - ing that He can - not do.

224 Reach Out and Touch the Lord

B. H.

BILL HARMON

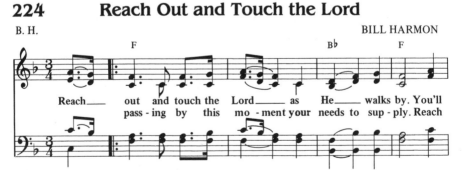

Reach out and touch the Lord as He walks by. You'll
pass - ing by this mo - ment your needs to sup - ply. Reach

find He's not too bus-y to hear your cry. He's
out and touch the Lord___ as

He walks by.

225 When We See Christ

E. K. R.

ESTHER KERR RUSTHOI

It will be worth it all ___ when we see Je - sus;___

Life's trials will seem so small___ when we see Christ!

___ One glimpse of His dear face___ all sor - row will e - rase;___

___ So brave-ly run the race___ till we see Christ.___

226 It Matters to Him

A. M.

AUDREY MIEIR

It mat-ters— to Him a-bout you;— Your heart-aches, your sor-row He shares.— Re-gard-less of what you may do,— He wants you, He loves you, He cares.— Oh, yes, it mat-ters— to Him a-bout you;— Be-lieve it be-cause it is

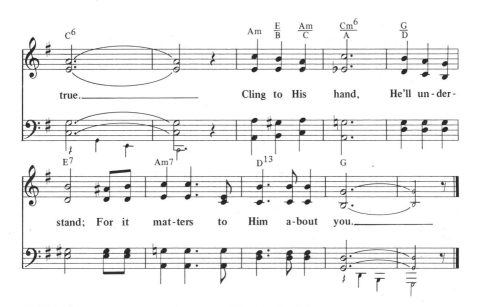

true._____ Cling to His hand, He'll under-
stand; For it mat-ters to Him a-bout you._____

227   Come, Holy Spirit

W. J. and GLORIA GAITHER   WILLIAM J. GAITHER

Come, Ho-ly Spir-it, I need You;_____ Come, sweet
Spir-it, I pray._____ Come, in Your strength and Your
pow-er;_____ Come, in Your own gen-tle way._____

228 God Said It, I Believe It, That Settles It

S. R. A. and GENE BRAUN

STEPHEN R. ADAMS

Lyrics:

God said it and I be-lieve it, And that set-tles it for me! God said it and I be-lieve it, And that set-tles it for me! Though some may doubt that His Word is true, I've cho-sen to be-lieve it; now how a-bout you? God said it and I be-lieve it, And that set-tles it for me!

Philippians 4:13

H. W. G.

HOMER W. GRIMES

230 When the Battle's Over

HARRIETTE WATERS

A. E. LIND

And when the bat-tle's o - ver, we shall wear a crown! Yes, we shall wear a

crown! Yes, we shall wear a crown! And when the bat-tle's o-ver, we shall wear a

crown In the new Je-ru-sa-lem. Wear a crown, Wear a crown,

wear a crown, Wear a bright and shin-ing crown. And wear a crown,

231 Let Go and Let God Have His Way

H. D. C.

HARRY D. CLARKE

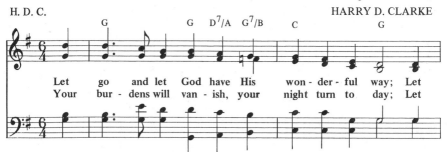

Let go and let God have His won-der-ful way; Let
Your bur - dens will van - ish, your night turn to day; Let

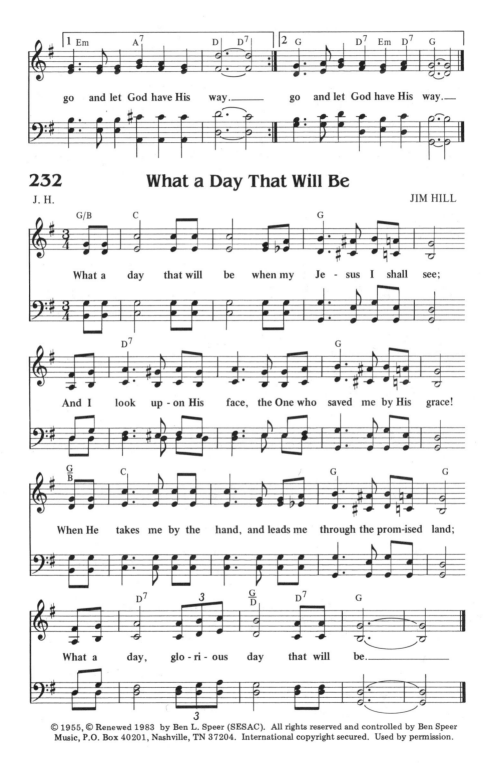

232 **What a Day That Will Be**

J. H.

JIM HILL

go and let God have His way.

go and let God have His way.

What a day that will be when my Je-sus I shall see;

And I look up-on His face, the One who saved me by His grace!

When He takes me by the hand, and leads me through the prom-ised land;

What a day, glo-ri-ous day that will be.

233 I Have Christ in My Heart

W. P. L.

WENDELL P. LOVELESS

Martial tempo

What though wars may come, with march-ing feet and beat of the drum? For
I have Christ in my heart. What though na-tions rage as
(my heart.) we ap-proach the end of the age? For I have Christ in my
heart. God is still on the throne, Al-might-y God is He;
And He cares for His own through all e-ter-ni-ty. So let

come what may; what - ev - er it is, I on - ly say That

I have Christ in my heart, I have Christ in my heart.

(in my heart,)

234   Give Them All to Jesus

BOB BENSON, SR., and P. J.   PHIL JOHNSON

Give them all, give them all, give them all___ to Je-

___ sus: Shat-tered dreams, wound-ed hearts,___ and bro-ken toys._____

- sus;___ And He will turn your sor - row___ in-to joy!_____

235 One of Your Children Needs You, Lord

M. L.

MOSIE LISTER

1. One of Your chil - dren needs You, Lord. One of Your
2. One of Your chil - dren is cry - ing, Lord. One of Your
3. One of Your chil - dren loves You, Lord. One of Your

chil - dren needs You, Lord. One of Your chil - dren
chil - dren is cry - ing, Lord. One of Your chil - dren is
chil - dren loves You, Lord. One of Your chil - dren

needs You, Lord.
cry - ing, Lord. Je - sus, Je - sus, be near._____
loves You, Lord.

Come to Me, all who are weary and heavy-laden, and I will give you rest.
Take My yoke upon you, and learn from Me, for I am gentle and humble in heart;
and you shall find rest for your souls.
For My yoke is easy, and My load is light (Matthew 11:28-30).

236 Right Now

O. S.

OTIS SKILLINGS

Right now, right now, com - mit your life_right now._____ De -

cide to live___your life for Him right now, right now.

237　Where the Spirit of the Lord Is

S. R. A.

STEPHEN R. ADAMS

Where the Spir-it of the Lord is, there is peace.

Where the Spir-it of the Lord is, there is love.

There is com-fort in life's dark-est hour, there is light and life; There is

help and pow-er in the Spir-it, in the Spir-it of the Lord.___

238   # Nothing Is Impossible

E. L. C.

EUGENE L. CLARK

Noth-ing is im - pos- si - ble when you put your trust in God;
Noth-ing is im - pos- si - ble when you're trust-ing in His Word.
Heark-en to the voice of God to thee:_____ "Is there an-y-thing too
hard for Me?" Then put your trust in God a - lone and
rest up-on His Word; For ev - 'ry-thing, O ev - 'ry-thing,

239

My Faith Still Holds

W. J. G. and GLORIA GAITHER

WILLIAM J. GAITHER

My faith still holds on to the Christ of Cal - va - ry;

Oh, bless - ed Rock of A - ges, cleft for me.

I glad - ly place my trust in things I can - not see;

My faith still holds on to the Christ of Cal - va - ry!

240

Gentle Shepherd

W. J. and GLORIA GAITHER

WILLIAM J. GAITHER

1, 3. Gen-tle Shep-herd, ___ come and lead us, ___ For we need You to help us
2. Gen-tle Shep-herd, ___ come and feed us, ___ For we

find our way. ___ need Your strength from day to day. ___ There's no

oth-er ___ we can turn to ___ Who can help us face an-oth-er day. ___

241

Greater Is He That Is in Me

Adapted from 1 John 4:4 by L. W.

LANNY WOLFE

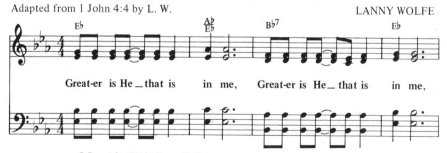

Great-er is He ___ that is in me, Great-er is He ___ that is in me,

Great-er is He__ that is in me Than he that is in__ the world!

The apostles said to the Lord, "Increase our faith!"
And the Lord said, "If you had faith like a mustard seed,
you would say to this mulberry tree, 'Be uprooted and be planted in the sea';
and it would obey you" (Luke 17:6).

242   Faith in God Can Move a Mountain

J. W. P. and A. E. S.   JOHN W. PETERSON and ALFRED E. SMITH

Faith in God can move a might-y moun-tain, Faith can
calm the trou-bled sea, Faith can make the
des-ert like a foun-tain, Faith can bring__ the vic-to-ry.

243 We've Come This Far by Faith

A. G.

ALBERT GOODSON

We've come this far___ by faith, lean-ing on the Lord,

Trust-ing in His ho-ly Word; He's nev-er failed___ us yet.

Oh,_____ we can't turn back; we've come this far ___ by faith!

244 I Believe the Answer's on the Way

M. D.

MERRILL DUNLOP

I be-lieve the an-swer's on the way; I be-lieve the
Now by faith in Him a-lone I stand, Firm-ly held by

Lord has heard me pray;___ "Cast not a-way your con-fi-dence,"
His al-might-y hand;___ Ful-ly___ trust-ing

saith the Lord our God.___ in His prom-ise, praise the Lord!

245   Cares Chorus

K. W.

KELLY WILLARD

I cast all my cares up-on You.___ I lay all of my

bur-dens down at Your feet.___ And an-y time that I don't know

what___ to do, I will cast all my cares___ up-on You.___

246   **He Will Carry You**

S. W. B.

SCOTT WESLEY BROWN

There is no prob - lem too big God can-not solve it.
There is no storm too dark God can-not calm it.

(solve it.)
(calm it.)
There is no moun - tain too tall He can-not
There is no sor - row too deep He can-not

move it.
(move it.)
soothe it.

REFRAIN

If He car-ried the weight of the world up-on His shoul-

247

There Is a River

DAVID and MAX SAPP

D. S. and M. S.

With a shuffle

There is a riv-er___ that flows from
(D.C.) Come to the wa-ter;___ there is a

deep with-in;___ There is a foun-tain___
vast sup-ply.___ There is a riv-er___

1 ___ that frees the soul from sin.___

2 ___ that nev-er shall run dry.___

248

Got Any Rivers?

OSCAR ELIASON

O. E.

Got an-y riv-ers you think are un-cross-a-ble? Got an-y moun-tains you
God spe-cial-iz-es in things thought im-pos-si-ble—

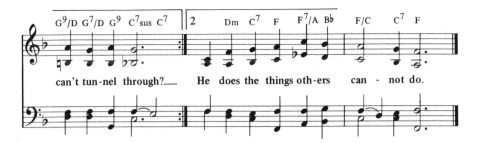

can't tun-nel through?___ He does the things oth-ers can - not do.

249   In the Name of the Lord

PHILL McHUGH, GLORIA GAITHER and S. P. H.   SANDI PATTI HELVERING

There is strength in the name of the Lord;___ There is

pow'r in the name of the Lord;___ There is

hope in the name of the Lord;___ Bless-ed is He___

___ who comes___ in the name of the Lord.___

250   He Is Our Peace

Eph. 2:14, 1 Pet. 5:7

KANDELA GROVES

He is our peace, who has bro-ken down ev-'ry wall.

He is our peace, He is our peace.

He is our peace. Cast all your cares on Him,

for He cares for you. He is our peace,

He is our peace. Cast all your peace.

TOPICAL INDEX

ALPHABETICAL INDEX